woman, child
for sale

The New Slave Trade
in the 21st Century

woman, child
for sale

The New Slave Trade
in the 21st Century

Gilbert King

Chamberlain Bros.
a member of Penguin Group (USA) Inc.
New York

Chamberlain Bros.
a member of
Penguin Group (USA) Inc.
375 Hudson Street
New York, NY 10014

LIBRARY OF CONGRESS CATALOGING-IN-PUBLICATION DATA
King, Gilbert.
  Woman, child for sale : the new slave trade in the 21st century / Gilbert
King.
    p. cm.
  Includes bibliographical references.
  ISBN 1-59609-005-7
  1. Prostitution. 2. Forced labor. 3. Child labor. 4. Slave trade. I. Title.
  HQ281.K56 2004   2004014729
  306.74—dc22

Printed in the United States of America

1 3 5 7 9 10 8 6 4 2

Book designed by Melissa Gerber.

Contents

Other titles by Gilbert King include:

Dirty Bomb: Weapon of Mass Disruption and

The Most Dangerous Man in the World: Dawood Ibrahim

Foreword

ELEANOR CLIFT,
AUTHOR OF *FOUNDING SISTERS*

"Slavery" is a loaded term. American society is still recovering from the abhorrent practice of one ethnic group holding another in forced servitude. We owe a debt of gratitude to President Lincoln for freeing the slaves, and to the 157,000 Americans who died in the Civil War as the North and South fought over the right to own slaves. To ignore history is to repeat it, which is why Gilbert King takes us back to the African slave trade to jolt us into seeing the similarities to what is happening in the world today. State-sanctioned slavery no longer exists, but there is a thriving black market in the trafficking of human beings. To supply a new global sex trade, every ten minutes a woman or girl somewhere in the developing world enters into a web of indentured labor. Some are lured by bait-and-switch schemes, after being promised a better life, but instead of receiving money for education, they sink into debt, forced to pay exorbitant fees for phony papers, unable to break out of bondage. In the developing world, where the majority of people barely eke out an existence, it's the law of supply and demand. A slave market flourishes to export human beings as cheap labor—men for the agricultural industry and women as domestic servants or prostitutes. Periodically, Americans are made aware of this unpleasant fact when one of the human-smuggling rings that brings workers across the ocean or across the border from Mexico is intercepted and the human cargo is discovered, often dead.

Globalization makes it easier to move people and goods around the world, which is why a modern-day slave trade is able to flourish undetected and untouched by the laws of individual nations. Senator Hillary Rodham Clinton calls it "the dark side of globalization." The same conditions that ease transactions between countries and bring us together as people also fuel the hatred that gives rise to terrorism and allows human traffickers to operate with impunity. The problem is serious enough that in a September 2003 speech to the United Nations, President Bush included alongside his case for waging war against Iraq a plea to the community of nations to acknowledge the estimated 800,000 to 900,000 human beings who are bought, sold, or forced across the world's borders each year. He singled out for special mention those who are victimized by the sex trade and said that "governments that tolerate this trade are tolerating a form of slavery."

Those are strong words, and some analysts have said Bush was only "playing to his base" by condemning the sex trade and likening it to slavery. At a time in American politics when partisan feelings are intense, such criticism is expected. But Bush also has nonpartisan allies on this issue, notably Senator Clinton. She urges her colleagues on Capitol Hill not to be fooled into thinking that the modern slave trade is just the normal pursuit of people seeking to better themselves, and that only moralists would object.

"They've got to understand that this is really at root a criminal enterprise that crosses all boundaries," she says. Modern-day slavery can't be eradicated with the stroke of a pen the way Lincoln did when he signed the Emancipation Proclamation. The world is more complicated today, and the solution to this problem is as elusive as the slavetraders themselves.

Prologue

The Beardens met the young Mexican girl while vacationing in Veracruz. She was bright and friendly, and her parents quickly recognized an opportunity for their only daughter. Divine intervention, perhaps. After all, Sandra Luz Bearden was a twenty-seven-year-old Mexican citizen herself, married to Warren Bearden, a man with a steady job and a comfortable house in Texas. This was the American dream knocking on the door. The Beardens convinced the girl's parents they could provide a better life for their daughter in America. They offered to take the twelve-year-old with them to Laredo, Texas, to work in their home as a maid, and offered food, clothing, a good education, and medical care in return. As a Mexican herself, Sandra Bearden presented a persuasive case for the American good life, and the girl's parents were convinced that they had secured a life-changing stroke of good fortune for their young daughter.

What unfolded in the next few months was nothing short of a nightmare. One of the Beardens' neighbors had heard strange noises coming from their house at odd hours of the night and called 911. When police arrived, they found the twelve-year-old shackled to a chain link fence in a small, caged area behind the Beardens' house. She had deep lacerations on her arms and legs where she was bound, and extensive bruising on her body and face. She was so dehydrated and malnourished that she could not stand. Sandra Bearden had sprayed mace into her eyes on several occasions.

Laredo police charged Sandra Bearden with aggravated kidnapping, injury to a child, and child abandonment. A few months later, she was convicted on seven counts and sentenced to ninety-nine years in prison after a jury deliberation of just five hours. The girl, (identified only by her initials, SAD) testified that Sandra Bearden regularly beat her with a belt, a broomstick, a glass, and even a skillet. Upon hearing of the jury's sentence in court, Sandra Bearden's mother, Lucy Carmen Quiroz-Orozco, sobbed and screamed at the panel, "Have mercy on her; she is a human being!"

This story of the enslaved child maid in Laredo, Texas is outrageous enough to make national headlines—no doubt made more shocking because the horror took place in an American suburb. But there are thousands more horror stories of human slavery each year in the United States. Many of these incidents stay below the radar of the mainstream media because they don't involve U.S. citizens. Or because the media continues, out of ignorance, to use the wrong word to describe teenage girls who are kidnapped, smuggled across borders, beaten, and raped into submission and forced into sexual slavery. The media calls them "prostitutes"—and in one quick breath, empathy, outrage, and the most basic human rights are obliterated. The world is simply unmoved by more stories of Russian "prostitutes" with pimp problems in the Balkans, or young Thai girls with HIV having unprotected sex in massage parlors in Bangkok, let alone New York or Chicago. What gets lost in these stories are the young, innocent lives snuffed out by violence and betrayal at the hands of someone they trusted, and sometimes by members of their own families. They do not choose to be workers in the sex trade. They are beaten and emotionally abused until they lose their will to resist. And their numbers are growing.

In a UN press release UNICEF Executive Director Carol Bellamy said, "We're talking about children who, instead of starting each day in the school yard, are getting up when it is still dark and toiling in slave-like conditions. This is not legitimate employment." Ms. Bellamy also stated that the children were deprived of education and proper medical care as well, and conditions were unacceptable. "Not only are these children being forced to work long, hard hours, but they are at increased risk of sexual abuse and being trafficked within and across borders."

Sandra Luz Bearden represents just a snapshot of

the new global slave traders. They prey on the most vulnerable—usually young women and children of poor families—with the promise of a better life in a richer country. But unlike Sandra Bearden, the most successful and prolific slave traffickers in the world deal with thousands of women and children and are rarely caught. And if caught, they are smart enough to stay in countries where officials can be bought off and where laws and cultural attitudes toward women insure a low risk of prosecution. The profit potential of forced slavery is at its greatest when there are weak economies and war in destabilized regions. These are very good times for human traffickers.

"There's another humanitarian crisis spreading, yet hidden from view. Each year, an estimated 800,000 to 900,000 human beings are bought, sold or forced across the world's borders."

"There's a special evil in the abuse and exploitation of the most innocent and vulnerable. The victims of {the} sex trade see little of life before they see the very worst of life—an underground of brutality and lonely fear. Those who create these victims and profit from their suffering must be severely punished. Those who patronize this industry debase themselves and deepen the misery of others. And governments that tolerate this trade are tolerating a form of slavery."

—President George W. Bush
Speech to the United Nations
New York City
September 23, 2003

TRAFFICKING IN PERSONS
A GUIDE FOR NON-GOVERNMENTAL ORGANIZATIONS

Pamphlet on "Trafficking in Persons",
U.S. Department of Justice, Washington, D.C., 2004

Introduction

On June 14th, 2004, the U.S. State Department issued its annual report on human trafficking. Once again, the numbers (600,000 to 800,000 persons trafficked across international borders each year for the sex trade and forced labor), according to Secretary of State Colin Powell, "can be numbing," he said. "They can freeze our imaginations."

Powell shifted the focus onto the individual cases in an effort to humanize the crisis. "We're talking about women and girls," he said, "as young as six years old, trafficked into commercial sexual exploitation; men trafficked into forced labor; children trafficked as child soldiers."

Nowhere is the scourge of human trafficking more abundant than in the developing world, where millions of children are exploited for domestic labor. According to a UN press release (10 Million Children Exploited for Domestic Labor, June 14th, 2004), country surveys indicate about 700,000 children are domestic workers in Indonesia alone, while there are also large numbers in Brazil (559,000), Pakistan (264,000), Haiti (250,000), Kenya (200,000) and Sri Lanka (100,000).

Whether it's domestic labor or the commercial sex trade, the numbers show that 70 percent of those who are trafficked across international borders are women, and 50 percent are children. "The more you learn about the most vulnerable among us who are savaged by these crimes," said Powell, "the harder it is to look the other way ..."

The 2004 report also examines the growing phenomenon of Child Sex Tourism, which involves people who travel from their home country to a foreign one to engage in commercial sex with children. The exploitation affects millions of children each year on every continent, as sex tourists from Japan and Europe travel to Thailand and Americans travel to Mexico or Central America. The global community is beginning to wake up to this horrific crime which is fueled by a combination of inconsistent and sometimes nonexistent law enforcement, the internet, and the disparity between wealthy and third world nations. "Operation Predator," a 2003 initiative to fight child exploitation, child pornography and child sex tourism, has been somewhat effective in attacking the demand side, as some twenty-five Americans were arrested last year for child sex tourism offenses.

What gets lost, year after year as these statistics and the stories of human exploitation are made public, are the many threats that human trafficking poses to all nations. Forced prostitution has led to an explosion in HIV and other communicable diseases such as tuberculosis, which presents serious public health concerns. Profits from trafficking are flowing directly into the hands of international crime syndicates which only serve to promote government corruption. This has a negative impact on labor markets, creating an endless cycle of poverty and illiteracy that stalls economic development in countries where human trafficking thrives.

However, it doesn't begin to address the price victims of human trafficking pay. Victims often experience physical and psychological harm, including disease, stunted growth, permanent damage to their reproductive organs, and post traumatic stress disorder in addition to the violence they are subjected to by their captors. Many are subdued with drugs, and children often miss critical opportunities for social, moral and spiritual development.

Human trafficking tears children away from their parents and family at a crucial time in their nurturing and development. They miss the chance at an education, so victims who are fortunate enough to return to their communities are often stigmatized and ostracized and have no opportunities for employment. As Colin Powell stated, slave traders prey on the world's most vulnerable—women and children in poverty who are usually tricked or coerced under the premise of marriage, employment, educational opportunities or a better life. Others are just violently abducted.

In an interview with Jamie Rubin for *Wide Angle* (PBS, *Dying to Leave*, September 25, 2003) Senator Hillary Rodham Clinton emphasized the magnitude of the crisis of human trafficking. "It's just heartbreaking and outrageous that, in the 21st century, we would see anyone treated like that. But it particularly reflects the continuing disregard of women's rights and the way that women are considered somehow less than human in many parts of the world and how they are used for sexual purposes without any regard to their human dignity and rights." She went on to say, ". . . this is perhaps the most fundamentally outrageous misuse of women, and to me it's an issue that speaks volumes about how far we still have to go in making sure that women's rights truly are human rights and are respected everywhere."

I.

HUMAN TRAFFICKING

CASE STUDIES IN MODERN SLAVERY AND EXPLOITATION

Every ten minutes, a woman or child is trafficked into the United States for forced labor. Around the world, it is estimated that twenty-seven million people are living in slavery, and human trafficking has become a $12 billion a year global industry. The numbers are staggering, yet they produce a numbing effect on the collective consciousness of us all. How could it be that there are twice as many people enslaved today than were enslaved in an African slave trade that lasted centuries? How could it be that as the CIA estimated in 1999, nearly 50,000 forced slaves are coming into America each year? And what exactly is human trafficking?

Human trafficking is the movement of people to

places for the purpose of forced labor, such as prostitution or migrant and domestic work. It is considered slavery because traffickers use deception, violence, threats, and other forms of coercion to force their victims to meet the high demand for commercial sex and cheap labor. It is a brutal and violent world that preys on the most vulnerable women and children from poor countries. Corruption among law enforcement officials and government agencies also plays a key role in the successful operation of the criminal networks that traffic in human slave labor.

"As I learned more and more about this issue it became abundantly clear that this issue was not limited to one particular region of the world. In addition, I found that human trafficking was not exclusively a crime of sexual exploitation. Taken independently, sex trafficking is an egregious practice in and of itself. It is also important, however, to be aware that people are being illegally smuggled across borders to work in sweatshops, domestic servitude, or other slavery-like conditions," said Congresswoman Louise M. Slaughter (N.Y.) in July of 2001.

"Human trafficking today is more profitable than ever before. Today, the profitability of these smuggling rackets rivals that of the drug trade. An estimated profit of $8 to $10 billion annually is garnered through prostitution and forced labor of those trafficked. The global sex trade, in particular, has boomed. In Japan, the world's second largest economy, the sex trade brings in $400 million per year," said Senator Sam Brownback (KS), in a press conference and release on September 24, 2003.

"Human trafficking is the 'perfect crime.' The chances of being caught are slight, small penalties exist for those unfortunate enough to be caught, huge profits can be made, and this particular trade rests on a commodity that can be used and reused, sold and bartered. The supply side of the equation is particularly bleak. While there are 100,000 places in the developed world for refugee resettlement per year, 50 million refugees and displaced persons exist worldwide today. This ready reservoir of the stateless presents an opportunity rife for exploitation by human traffickers," Senator Brownback added.

U.S. Attorney General John Ashcroft stated in 2003, "Those who traffic in human lives treat people as easily expendable and highly profitable. But behind each dollar sign is a human tragedy."

In an effort to put human faces on the millions of women and children who are exploited each year, the following are selective case studies that illustrate this broad range of abuse on a global scale:

YULIA: RUSSIA

She was a normal teenager living a normal teenage life with normal teenage worries—the stresses of college life, a new boyfriend, and a job that never paid enough for her to really enjoy what little free time she had. Tall, thin, blonde, and attractive, Yulia met a boy who seemed to like everything about her, and they became very close. She even danced for him in private, which drove him wild. That's when her boyfriend started getting ideas. In Russia, opportunities to make money were few and far between. But Yulia could dance. Her boyfriend knew of an agency that offered young Russian women work abroad as waitresses, dancers, or nannies. The money would be extraordinary, he told her, and she could work for a while, then return to Russia to finish college with some money in the bank. Yulia couldn't see anything wrong with the plan, and she agreed to dance abroad. But almost right away, she knew something was very wrong.

After signing up for the agency, she was locked up in a dilapidated building with dozens of teenage girls, threatened and forced to work as a prostitute. According to an Associated Press story, Yulia's captors told her she owed thousands of dollars in airfare and job-placement fees, and unless she did as she was told, her parents would be responsible for the payments and might possibly get hurt. It was too much for the nineteen-year-old Russian girl to contemplate, so she complied with the demands of her captors. For the next several months, Yulia lived a nightmarish existence. She was kept in a cold, run down house with no hot water and bars on the windows, preventing her escape. A video camera tracked all the movements of the women in the building, and they were only allowed to step outside the house for thirty minutes a day—and had a hefty fine waiting for them if they stayed outside longer.

"There were fines for everything; if you looked sad when you sat at the bar, if you went to the bathroom for longer than five minutes, if you tried to refuse to go with a man," Yulia told Dolgov.

Yulia went on to say that two other Russian girls in the house were killed in the time she was there. She survived. But she does not consider herself lucky. She returned to Russia, "still pretty," according to Dolgov, but "she looks much older than her nineteen years, with dull pain and suffering in her eyes."

Yulia dropped out of college and had no money to show for her three-month ordeal. She told Dolgov that her health was not good, but she did not want to elaborate. She is one of the growing number of "Natashas"—the term for these omnipresent East European girls who are forced into the sex trade.

SIRI: THAILAND

What happened to Siri, a young girl born in northeastern Thailand, is an all-too-frequent occurrence in Southeast Asia, where traffickers arrive at very poor villages with great sums of money and the worst of intentions. In his book, *Disposable People: New Slavery in the Global Economy*, author Kevin Bales illustrates Siri's case, which is typical in small areas of rural Thailand. Siri grew up normally enough, attending four years of school before her parents needed her to stay home to help care for her three younger siblings. When she turned fourteen, a well-dressed woman arrived in the village, offering Siri's parents $2,000 so that Siri could take a "good job" in a larger town.

Siri had a short but painful flight from innocent Thai farmgirl to debt slave in the sex industry. The trafficker "sold" Siri to a brothel in another town, where Siri was "initiated" into prostitution by a pimp who raped her shortly after meeting her. Siri's very first client also abused her, and after that she escaped the brothel, turning to a policeman for help. But as is the case in many third world countries, the police are often paid off by the brothels, and Siri was returned to her pimp for yet another beating.

As punishment for her attempted escape, Siri's debt was doubled from $4,000 to $8,000, which she was forced to repay from her share of her "earnings" per customer, which was just four dollars. To cover her rent, Siri had to sexually service three hundred men each month before she could begin to cut into her debt—a helpless situation that forced her to actually befriend her pimp to survive. It did not take long for the pimp to convince Siri of her worthlessness, and for Siri to accept the view of herself as a mere female who deserved her fate because of past life sins. Siri became psychologically enslaved, and ultimately spent her downtime in her brothel room, praying to Buddha to protect her from HIV and other sexually transmitted diseases.

THE CADENAS: UNITED STATES

When agents from both the FBI and the U.S. Border Patrol conducted simultaneous raids on six brothels in Florida in November 1997, they uncovered evidence of an organized and extensive prostitution ring that reached as far north as South Carolina. At the heart of the ring was the Cadena-Sosa family—a closely knit extended family from southeastern Mexico that preyed on young and naïve Mexican girls and smuggled them into migrant-farmworker camps, where they were forced to have sex with migrant workers in trailers set up as brothels.

In a familiar scheme, the young girls from small towns near Veracruz were lured by well-dressed Cadena women with promises of jobs in the United States that did not exist. Antonia Sosa, the mother of the four Cadena-Sosa brothers, and Carment Cadena, wife of Juan Luis Cadena, appeared successful to the parents of these young victims, and when the Cadena women told the parents they needed waitresses for the family business or nannies for their sons and brothers in Florida, there was no reason for the parents to believe they were lying. The girls were assured that they would be earning hundreds of dollars each week, plus tips, which in just weeks would easily offset the $2,000 in smuggling costs. The Cadena recruiters assured the sometimes-nervous parents that the girls would be safe in their care and made it a point to tell them that the girls could always return to Mexico if they were not happy.

Florida State University's Center for the Advancement of Human Rights report, titled, "Florida Responds to Human Trafficking" reported that the Cadenas would then smuggle the girls, many as young as 14 years old, across the Rio Grande River and into Texas, where they were then taken to Florida in vans. Soon after the girls arrived in Florida, the vicious beatings and rapes began at the hands of the Cadenas and their associates, who viewed the violence as necessary in order to increase a girl's production in the sex trade she was about to enter. Some of the young girls who came to Florida in vans were virgins, and they were "taught" to have sex by being raped by the Cadena brothers themselves.

Once the girls were settled in Florida, they were sent to various migrant camps to sexually service workers in run-down houses and trailers, usually located in remote rural areas. The migrant workers were charged $20 for fifteen minutes with the girls, and the Cadenas frequently rotated the girls between brothels. This strategy was designed to keep the girls in the dark as to their physical location, and to provide johns with new girls on a regular basis. It also prevented clients from becoming too involved with any of the girls, since they often moved on to new brothels without any advance notice.

"We worked six days a week and twelve hour days," said "Maria," one of the girls enslaved by the Cadenas in her testimony to a U.S. Senate subcommittee in April 2000. "We mostly had to serve thirty-two to thirty-five clients a day. Our bodies were utterly sore and swollen."

Any resistance would lead to severe beatings, rapes, and confinement in dark closets at gunpoint for days at a time. The Cadenas also told the girls that their families back in Mexico would be killed if they tried to escape.

Ultimately, eight members of the Cadena-Sosa family were convicted, with ringleader Rogerio Cadena pleading guilty to civil-rights violations and sentenced to fifteen years in a U.S. prison. The Cadenas were ordered to repay the women, but they pleaded poverty, despite the fact that they had earned several million dollars in profits, enabling them to acquire substantial real estate holdings in Mexico. Seven of the indicted Cadenas successfully made it back to Mexico and avoided prosecution.

ANASTASIA: INTERNET MAIL-ORDER BRIDE

Anastasia Solovieva was a beautiful young woman from Kyrgyzstan who came to Seattle, Washington, as a teenage internet mail-order bride. Her prospective husband-to-be, Indle King—a divorced man twice her age—had seen her pictures and began e-mailing the tall blonde. After a trip to Kyrgyzstan, he promised her a superb education and a better life in America as his bride. Anastasia arrived in the United States with King, and for a while, she was living the American dream. She was enrolled in the University of Washington and began making close friends with young women her age in the Seattle area. But before long, the young Russian began to suspect that her husband had a few secrets, and she worried that her dream was in danger.

Anastasia learned about King's first wife, Yekaterina

Kazakova—another Russian who ended up divorcing King after a short marriage, and who, in King's view, fleeced him in the settlement. Indle King was determined not to let that happen to him again, and at the slightest hint of marital strife he was prepared to go to any lengths to prevent another divorce.

When Anastasia disappeared after she left her parents' house in the former Soviet republic of Kyrgyzstan in September 2000, King told police that his mail-order bride had "dumped" him in Moscow during their trip. However, U.S. customs records showed that King and his wife had both returned from Russia, passing through the Sea-Tac International Airport together. But the missing-persons case would soon take an odd turn when an inmate at the Snohomish County Jail, twenty-one-year-old Daniel Larson, began getting visits from Indle King, and the authorities decided to investigate. Upon questioning, Larson told police that King had killed his wife and led detectives to Anastasia's body, which was buried under a mattress in a dump in nearby Tulalip Indian Reservation.

Larson would later testify in court that he and King were lovers, and that the two killed the young Russian together, with King sitting on his wife's chest while Larson strangled her. King's trial would also show that King was obsessed with holding on to his money in the event of another divorce, and he went to great lengths to deceive Anastasia, such as hiding her passport and papers during a trip to Kyrgyzstan, hoping she would be prevented from returning to the United States. When his computer was confiscated for evidence, it was discovered that King had begun corresponding with yet another mail-order bride just three weeks before he killed Anastasia. King would ultimately be convicted and sentenced to nearly thirty years in prison.

LATIFA: MOROCCO

When Latifa was eight years old, her father became seriously ill. He could no longer hold a paying job, and had no pension or any other source of income. And so began Latifa's working life. According to Dr. June Kane in a landmark new study entitled "Helping Hands or Shackled Lives" (ILO, CH-1211 Geneva 22,

Switzerland, 2004) Latifa's first job was to work for a civil servant and his wife, acquaintances of her father. They had recently borne a child, and Latifa was to help the wife with the chores surrounding the baby. "The father decided Latifa should go to live with them. Latifa tells that, every day, the husband asked Latifa to do a little more," wrote Dr. Kane. "Soon she was washing clothes, doing the dishes, running errands and other duties . . . Latifa recalls that she often had to wash clothes on the roof terrace, even when it was raining, with her feet and hands in the water for a long time. As an eight-year-old, she did not manage to do this properly . . . The wife soon started to beat her."

SHIRWA: TANZANIA

"I have been a victim of prostitution because I have no-one to help and support," Dr. Kane quoted Shirwa as saying. After a very long and protracted illness, Shirwa's mother died when Shirwa was seven years old. She was certain that her father's mother had bewitched the deceased mother, with whom she had fought bitterly for many years. Shirwas left home when she was nine years old, and became a domestic servant. "During my stay with my employer, at the age of 13, I was made pregnant by my lady lord's brother who refused to take any responsibility. The family supported me during my late pregnancy, maybe because I was working. I was told to leave 30 days after the delivery. It was very difficult to go home. I found myself here through my friend. I work for an elder lady helping her to sell kimpumu [a local tribal brew]. I earn nothing. I am given food and shelter."

FATOU: SENEGAL

Fatou Ndiaye was born in Monbaye to desperately poor parents. She left her home and family at the age of seven to seek a better life in Dakar, the nearest town. Upon entering the city, she immediately faced several dangers. "I came to the city in 1991. I was so small. I knew next to nothing. In the village I carried water, gathered wood. Work is very different here in town. I looked after babies, earning around 2,000 francs (US $3.60) a month. Sometimes I had kind employers; others beat me," Dr. Kane quoted Fatou.

Fatou did her work and progressed nicely as a house servant. She could be trusted to wash, sweep and iron by the age of thirteen years old, and by fifteen years of age she was earning more than 10,000 F (US $18) per month. With this salary, she was able to support her mother and two younger siblings. And she was also able to return home once a year to her village for the annual festival. By all accounts, Fatou thought her employers kind.

According to Dr. Kane, Fatou later joined a workers union that informed them of their rights as citizens and how to organize in support of one another. They have instituted literacy classes, health insurance, and a network to identify higher paying positions within the region.

"We worked during all last year for five rights: the right to learn a trade; to read, to write; to organize; and the right to demand self-respect . . . They dare no longer mistreat us," she stated in Dr. Kane's book.

GLORIA: PHILIPPINES
In the Philippine city of Pasig, Gloria, a thirteen-year-old girl, entered a household as a domestic worker in

order to earn enough money to complete her secondary education back in her small village. However, her dreams were shattered when her mother, Chedita, re-married and began garnishing 75% of the wages she was earning, instantly depriving her of any hopes of resuming her schooling.

"Five months later Gloria was told to take care of an epileptic adult daughter of her employer. Already struggling to complete all the other domestic chores, Gloria was unable to cope with the sick woman. Her employers hit her for not taking proper care of their child," Dr. Kane reported. "Gloria's beatings worsened following an incident when the epileptic woman fell and hurt herself during a seizure. A child, brimful of guilt and fear, Gloria faced her punishments in silence."

One day, Chedita finally saw the brutal treatment her daughter was suffering. Gloria was being severely whipped. "Chedita begged for the employers to release her daughter, but they refused. The beatings became more frequent," wrote Dr. Kane.

Eventually Chedita helped to free her daughter by

reporting her employers to the government, and Gloria was removed. Chedita was too poor to care for her child, so Gloria was placed in a shelter and was provided counseling, while her former employers faced charges brought on by the local authorities.

SANTA EVA: GUATEMALA

Santa Eva was born in Guatemala. She and her three brothers were abandoned by their mother when they were still in their formative years. Their mother had left the family to marry another man, and Santa Eva had to provide for her brothers. She was heartbroken, and spoke later of "the 'torture' of seeing her mother who lived only two blocks away with her new family while she and her brothers were abandoned. At times, she saw her mother in the market and was mistreated when she tried to speak to her," wrote Dr. Kane. Santa Eva worked in a tortilla making factory, as a packager of vegetables in an export company, and became a domestic servant all before the age of twelve years old. At that time, "after a long and difficult year, her health began to deteriorate."

"Santa Eva was saved when she was twelve years old by the facilitator of the Conrado de la Cruz Association action program against child domestic labor," Dr. Kane went on to write. Soon, in shelters run by the program, Santa Eva found other girls who had suffered similar experiences, and found some measure of comfort among her peers. "Santa has also recovered her physical and mental health through this program, as well as being able to study and have hope for the future. She was able to finish her primary education. . .

Today, Santa is fifteen years old and she works for the association as a group presenter, participates in classes at the Education Centre, has done a computer course and is studying to be a nursing assistant," concluded Dr. Kane.

COMMONWEALTH OF THE NORTHERN MARIANA ISLANDS

In May 1999, U.S. Senator Daniel K Akaka (HI) pointed out a scandal in the American Commonwealth of the Northern Mariana Islands. Senator Akaka exposed the story of a tropical paradise destroyed by greed and corruption through forced labor and sex trade workers.

"In the Commonwealth of the Northern Mariana Islands, foreign workers have been imported en masse to assemble goods for export to the United States. Taking advantage of loopholes in our immigration and labor laws, foreign businessmen use the Mariana Islands as a base to export garments to the United States. These foreign businessmen pay no export taxes, and their goods are not subject to textile quotas. Their workers are paid below minimum wage levels, if paid at all, and often live in deplorable conditions," said Senator Akaka.

He was quick to show that women from Asia and Russia were being imported with the promise of high-paying jobs in the United States only to find themselves marooned. With no way to escape, they were forced to work as prostitutes in the flourishing Mariana sex trade.

Citing a report filed by the television news magazine 20/20, entitled "Trapped: Human Trafficking for Forced Labor in The Commonwealth of The Northern Mariana Islands," the report illustrated the disturbing details that involved trafficking of humans for indentured labor in factories and sex trade emporiums in the Marianas. The report alleged that organized crime groups from Japan, South Asia, and the People's Republic of China had enslaved approximately forty thousand indentured workers "in the CNMI, earning about $160 million in profits for criminal syndicates."

"Indentured workers are being used to manufacture ostensibly 'Made in the USA' garments for export to the United States. None of these goods are required to be shipped to the U.S. on U.S.-flagships in accordance with the Jones Act," the Senator asserted. He also fumed that these practices were making this "former tropical paradise a major center for the booming Asian sex trade. Women from Asia and Russia are being lured to the Northern Marianas with promises of work opportunities in the United States, only to find themselves imprisoned on islands from which there is no escape unless they agree to their employer's demands that they become prostitutes and sex hostesses. This sick trade in prostitution must be stopped." He also entreated his fellow Senators to join him "in ending this deplorable situation in which men and women are being used virtually as slaves on an American commonwealth."

While arrests on the islands were made before and after this speech was given, the sex trade has only been weakened, not eradicated.

100 SLAVES – LONG ISLAND, NEW YORK

At 5 a.m. on June 21, 2004, Peruvian immigrants who were living in virtual servitude and afraid of deportation were startled to a frenzy when U.S. Federal immigration officials staged a dawn raid freeing the victims. Federal authorities alleged that Mariluz Zavala (forty-two years old), her husband, Jorge Ibanez (forty-one years old), and their daughter Evelyn Ibanez (twenty years old) had been running a smuggling and slavery operation for almost four years out of their own small home and two other homes, all of which were tucked into the quiet streets of suburban Long Island, New York. Some victims, split between the small houses, were forced to live in a tool shed or in garages with no toilets or running water.

Authorities liberated sixty-nine Peruvian nationals

(thirteen of which were children) who were being detained in servitude and paid little or no wages. They came to the country seeking employment, but were met with something even uglier. The same people who promised them jobs ended up confiscating their paychecks, under the threat of deportation. The workers would not receive payment until they worked off "fees" being charged to them for their transportation into the country. The family charged each person anywhere from $6,000 to $7,500. The family also added surcharges for room, boarding, and transportation, leaving each person with little or no money. In many cases, the visas that were fraudulent to begin with were confiscated from the abused individuals. Many of the victims worked in nearby factories and other area businesses. They got these jobs via phony Social Security cards and forged documents, all of which were supplied by Ibanez.

"These aliens were held in virtual servitude as they paid off their debts, proving that smugglers are more interested in profits than people," said Martin Ficke, special agent in charge for the U.S. Immigration and

Customs Enforcement bureau, in a statement on the day of the arrests.

"Criminals who smuggle aliens exploit human misery and take advantage of families in desperate financial straits who will go to any length to come to the United States," said U.S. Attorney Roslynn Mauskopf.

PEOPLE FOR SALE IN CANADA?

It is estimated that the annual revenues from illegal trafficking in human beings generates approximately $120 to $400 million dollars (Canadian). In particular, the Vietnamese and the Chinese mafias bring anywhere from 8,000 to 16,000 women and children into Canada each year, according to the "Organized Crime Impact Study" from the Solicitor General of Canada, Canadian Department of Justice (April 2004).

The influx of women and children, particularly from Southeast Asia, has seen huge increases in operations. According to Rob Lamberti in "Sex Slaves: Fodder for Flesh Factories the Women Earn Nothing But Tips Until They Pay Off Their $40,000 Contracts," *Toronto Sun*, 10 May 1998, recruiters can get approximately $8,000 per girl from the securing agents, who then in turn resell them to pimps in local markets who buy them for $15,000. Canadian officials tell stories of young women who were forced to work twelve-hour days, who must service approximately four hundred customers to pay off their debts to their pimps. Women are repeatedly beaten and terrorized. Some were even scorched with hot irons.

Lamberti's story told of trips that were regularly made into Toronto and surrounding environs, wherein at least thirty Thai women and girls from the ages of sixteen to thirty were brought in per trip. The Toronto area alone is known to have three Thai agents who in turn sell the girls to the local brothels.

These recruiting rings are not just made up of foreigners. There are plenty of citizens who are not immune to the desire for quick riches at any cost. One infamous ring was Canadian-family run. A man and his wife, their son, daughter, and daughter-in-law all recruited young foreign women who were forced into the sex trade for a profit of more than $1.2 million (Canadian) in a two year span, according to George

Christopoulos. "Many of the twenty prostitutes—aged twenty-three to thirty-nine—were related to the operators by marriage or blood," said Sgt. Lino Murarotto of the 32nd Division, Toronto police force. "They worked out of apartments and each turned over at least $15,000 a year to the operators."

"Sadly, many people have found out, too late, that the promises made by traffickers were lies," reads a Canadian Department of Justice report. "This is what happened to them when traffickers brought them to Canada:

They were guarded at all times and could not go out on their own.

They were forced to have unprotected or dangerous sex with strangers.

They were threatened, beaten, raped or punished.

They did not get paid for the work they did.

They were not allowed to speak to other people or to make Canadian friends.

They were told they would have to work until their debt was paid and their debt kept getting bigger, not smaller.

They could not get medical services or help if they needed it.

They could not get away because they had been forced to break the law and were afraid.

Their families back home were threatened with violence or injury.

It is hard to get away from a trafficker. Traffickers know how to make people feel vulnerable and afraid. They know how to keep people trapped in a situation. They are part of an organized network. Please be careful. Traffickers profit from your work and they will not want to let you go."

Human trafficking has become so bad in North America that the Canadian government issued a poster warning of the perils of human trafficking. The government has urged its citizens not to fall for the many schemes as well as to be on the lookout for foreigners who they suspect of being victimized.

"I am pleased as well that we now have a poster for raising awareness and serving as a call to action," said Irwin Cotler, Minister of Justice and Attorney General of Canada. "This poster will be widely distributed and will go a long way to making sure that Canadians across the country realize that this modern slavery is not something 'out there' that doesn't touch us. It's something that exists here in Canada; and it not only touches us, but is part of an international connecting link—an assault for which we will need, as I say, a comprehensive strategy of cross-commitment."

SLAVES IN SOHO—LONDON

"If Tony Blair took a short stroll from Downing Street to Soho, the heart of London's sex trade, he'd find human rights abuses right under his nose every bit as terrible as those in Iraq," wrote Ros Coward.

Coward pointed to a sad story from the previous year, when an impoverished fifteen-year-old Romanian girl testified against her pimp in a London court. The girl was identified as "Natasha" (not coincidentally, the generic name given the throngs of young Russian and Eastern-European girls who are forced into the sex trade every year). "She had been forced to have sex with customers for twenty hours a day, earning her 'owner' £500 a day. She'd come from a broken and impoverished home in Romania, been tempted by offers of a better life, and ended up trafficked via the Balkans to sex slavery in London. A similar recent prosecution of two Albanians for trafficking, rape, indecent assault and drug possession revealed another Romanian girl, sixteen-year-old Anna, who had been sold at twelve and trafficked via Macedonia to London."

Estimated to run around a £12 million industry in Soho, London, the market is dominated by the Albanian mafia, who have won much local business by cutting service rates to their customers and taking it out in trade from their young, enslaved charges. In most cases the girls have been either duped or abducted, and once arrived in London, they are regularly beaten and abused.

"Teenage girls are being kidnapped and smuggled into Britain to be sold as sex slaves for £3,000 each. The terrified youngsters are held prisoner in brothels where they are forced into prostitution by their masters. *Sunday Mirror* investigators were offered the chance to buy 100 of the girls—three of them aged just 15," reported Graham Johnson and Dominic Hipkins in "Sex Slaves for Sale at £3,000 Each," which appeared in the December 28, 2003, *Sunday Mirror*.

Johnson and Hipkins reported at that time that illegal immigrant Luan Plakici, just twenty-six years old himself and an Albanian crime lord, had been convicted of smuggling up to sixty women into Britain who were later beaten and forced into the sex trade. Scotland Yard touted Plakici as one of the biggest Eastern European sex traffickers in London.

The two journalists were also reportedly offered other women. "We can send girls to Britain. You like Russian girls? We send each one for six months and you pay 5,000 euros (£3,000) each," Russian godfather Ima told the two *Sunday Mirror* reporters. Ima offered to supply 100 young Russian women who were either duped or kidnapped in Russia and brought to London.

In an earlier story filed by Johnson and Nyra Mahmood ("I Sell Kids for Sex," *Sunday Mirror*, January 6, 2002), trafficker Aktham Zuhair Salem Madanat boasted he could procure and deliver two young Cuban girls to Britain for just £500 each. The youngest was aged eleven. "The girls are barely out of puberty—11, 12, 13, 14—but they have the bodies of older women. Already by the time they are 10 or 11 . . . the way Cuban girls move their bodies . . . everything is for the pleasure of men. I can get them to London for about £500. They can earn that back in one week."

CONCLUSION

Whether they are abused as domestics, forced laborers, or as sexual slaves, the stories are unbearably heartbreaking. "This is modern-day slavery, and it should not be confused with any other cause, legitimate or illegitimate, that a local political leader might seize on . . . We're concerned about people who either are forcibly taken from their homes and sold into either sexual slavery or other kinds of servitude, hard labor..." U.S. Senator Hillary Rodham Clinton told Jamie Rubin of PBS's Wide Angle.

Women often find that they have been sold into or tricked into sexual servitude, often becoming sex workers by forced means. Nearly all are beaten, no matter the country they are incarcerated in, whether in the United States or elsewhere in the world. Few are brave enough to seek help from local authorities.

As recently as June 2004, the United Nations held a summit regarding children and servitude. "Up to 10 million children—mostly girls—are trapped in low-paid jobs as domestic servants, where they are at risk of sexual abuse, physical exploitation and human trafficking," reported the United Nations in a press release on June 14, 2004. The report went on to say, "These youngsters are usually 'invisible' to their communities, toiling for long hours with little or no pay and regularly deprived of the chance to play or go to school."

Children who serve as domestic laborers often suffer direct physical abuse. They are often beaten to insure their complicity in these heinous arrangements. Being slow or uncooperative, or making mistakes in their work will often lead to beatings, a recent International Labor Organization report cited. "They may be burned or otherwise tortured, and not only by the adult members of the family but by children in the family who see cruelty as a valid relationship with 'inferior' members of the household, or by other domestic helpers trying to impose a hierarchy even among those being exploited," wrote Dr. June Kane.

Dr. Kane went on to point out that female children were specifically at risk, although male children were not excluded from such abuses. According to studies, "in El Salvador, for example, 66.4 percent of the girls working in domestic service reported that they had been physically or psychologically abused, many of them sexually, and that the threat of sexual advances from their employers was always present." Not only were the girls at risk from older, powerful male masters, but "girl-children may be abused by adult men in the household or by older or stronger children. They may also be exposed to sexual abuse by visitors to the household, or by other domestic helpers," said Dr. Kane.

Many sexually abused young girls often wound up pregnant. Those children, once identified, often faced immediate expulsion, and were immediately expelled from the home in which they served and where they were the victim of abuse. Many were simply turned out into the street.

"As in all forms of sexual abuse of children, the child faces long-term repercussions of such exploitation. The impact on the reproductive health of girls whose bodies are not ready for sexual activity is severe. Beyond the risks of STD infection, they may suffer lesions that do not heal properly and complications from pregnancy, in addition to the psychological damage of sexual activity that is not understood or that causes shame or guilt," wrote Dr. Kane.

There are no easy answers. As these case studies prove, sometimes these are pure bait-and-switch practices run by grotesque traffickers, and sometimes servitude is the last refuge of well-meaning parents who cannot afford to feed their own children, and where relationships, slowly or suddenly, go very wrong.

Either way, this is the very essence of slavery and trafficking, and it cannot be equivocated.

"You can buy a woman for $10,000 and you can make your money back in a week if she is pretty and she is young. Then everything else is profit."

—*Convicted racketeer Ludwig Fainberg,*
in an interview with Victor Malarek, author of
The Natashas: The New Global Sex Trade

2.

THE TRAFFICKERS:

PROFILES OF NEW SLAVE TRADERS OF THE TWENTY-FIRST CENTURY

Those who trade in humans acquire their victims in different ways, depending on the area of the world in which they do their business. In Russia and Eastern Europe, victims are often lured from their homelands with the promise of phony job offers, such as dancing, domestic work, and positions as au pairs. Marriage agency databases and matchmaking agencies are also popular ruses for luring unsuspecting women into slavery. In other cases, women are kidnapped and taken by force across borders. In Sri Lanka and India, thousands of Nepalese girls are abducted each year for sexual exploitation in India.

Countries such as Thailand, Cambodia, and the

Philippines are often destinations for tourists who are intent on engaging in sexual acts with minors, and large-scale child prostitution rings flourish there. Needless to say, human trafficking has become a billion- dollar industry on a global scale, and the most successful and notorious traffickers have made themselves rich at the expense of the enslaved.

DILAVER "LEKU" BOJKU

Dilaver Bojku, one of the most well-known human traffickers in the world, got a small taste of what it was like to lose some basic human rights when he was arrested and imprisoned in Macedonia. He was charged with enslaving hundreds of young women from Eastern Europe and forcing them into the sex trade. Sentenced to a mere six months for trafficking, the little time Bojku spent behind bars in June 2003 was too much for the Macedonian Mafioso to bear. The man they call "Leku" took advantage of a poorly planned prison transfer to make his escape. Overpowering the lightly armed court police, Leku jumped into a waiting black car and drove off.

Leku's escape was viewed as a significant setback to efforts to stem the tide of women and girls trafficked in the Balkans—a number estimated at more than 200,000 each year. Hundreds had been forced into slavery and prostitution, with Leku as the undisputed "boss pimp" of the operation. Leku's escape also called attention to the government corruption that helped facilitate his involvement in the sex trade. And his imprisonment in a minimum-security facility where he was free to visit pubs and restaurants in town, then return to jail, seemingly for a night's sleep, has embarrassed Macedonian officials, who have been attempting to counter the negative image the West has of Macedonia. The United States quickly stepped in, offering a $10,000 reward for information leading to Leku's recapture, and on July 4, a police officer in Montenegro captured him in the town of Ulcinj while he was preparing to escape to Brazil.

Dilaver Bojku was ultimately returned to Macedonia where he was sentenced to three years and eight months in prison in December 2003. But left behind in the wake of Leku's business were countless young women who, if they survived, were struggling to pick up the pieces of their damaged lives. In a story by Zaklina Gorgevik for the Skopje daily *Utrinski Vesnik*, a twenty-one-year-old Romanian girl described how she was lured to Macedonia and forced into prostitution: "I was told that I would be found work in Greece, but I never thought I was being sold [to work as a prostitute]."

She had arrived in the village of Velesta, a small and lawless area of western Macedonia, where traffickers promised her a job as a waitress. But once there, she was handed over to Leku and forced to work as a prostitute in one of his bars.

"Some girls managed to escape," she said, "but they were caught, brought back and beaten. [Leku] gave us no money except on rare occasions when he was in a good mood. The clients paid 50 euro for every hour they spent with us."

Leku's modus operandi is typical among those who engage in human trafficking and the sex trade. Traffickers generally prey on the feelings of economic hopelessness that young women are exposed to in their homelands. Unemployment can be as high as 25 percent in many Eastern European countries, and the promise of waitressing or dancing jobs in wealthier countries represents a possibly significant change in fortune for many. According to the U.S. State Department's Bureau of Intelligence and Research report for the CIA, International Trafficking in Women to the United States: A Contemporary Manifestation of Slavery and Organized Crime by Amy O'Neill Richard, traffickers typically charge these young women highly inflated prices for securing alleged jobs, travel documentation, transportation, food and lodging, and other incidentals. In order to increase their profits, traffickers keep the women in poor, crowded conditions and feed them a steady diet of macaroni or rice, depending on the region, to keep costs down. The women's passports are usually confiscated, and they are forced to purchase them back from their captors at costs ranging from $900 to $4,000. But those costs do not buy a woman her freedom, as there are other debts that must be repaid as well.

Slave traders such as Leku make it a point to see a return on their investments as quickly as possible, and women are often beaten and raped into submission so that they can begin earning money as prostitutes the moment they reach their destinations. The women are expected to sexually service dozens of men each day. Long-term "production" from enslaved women is not a concern for traffickers, because they understand that they have just a few months to maximize the earning potential of these women before their health and youthful looks decline dramatically.

SLAVES OF NEW YORK:
ANOTHER RUSSIAN STORY

The women of Voronezh, Russia, a center of agricultural business, came to the United States to get jobs and to start a new life. That's what they were promised, but that's not what happened. When they arrived at Kennedy Airport in New York City with visas saying they were here for work, it was the last time they were actually free. Once they went through security and into a waiting van, they lost all freedom. Their visas were confiscated by force, and each woman was beaten. Much to their own personal shock and horror, they were to be strippers and prostitutes. Each was charged a "fee" of $5,000 which they would have to "earn" through credits, which were virtually impossible to pay off.

"At the center of the case involving the women of Voronezh is Lev Trakhtenberg, a thirty-nine-year-old Russian émigré who produces theatrical shows for Brighton Beach's Russian community," wrote Thomas Zambito of the *New York Daily News*. "Trakhtenberg arrived in the United States in 1992 with a master's degree in Russian literature and few prospects. Within a week, he found work outside the Democratic National Convention at Madison Square Garden, hawking flyers for a Manhattan strip club."

According to Federal prosecutors, in the 1990s, Trakhtenberg and his ex-wife, Viktoriya I'lina, came up with a plan to convince hard-pressed women in Russia that high-paying, respectable jobs in the U.S. were plentiful and for the taking. Their visa told of women who would be working as professional musicians or for the University of Illinois. However, their goal was to feed fresh new faces to a chain of strip clubs in New Jersey.

Newspapers in Voronezh were filled with offers of a better life and good work. Viktoriya's ex-boyfriend Sergey Malchikov, a former professional boxer, was hired to take the girls to and from their lightly furnished apartment in Brooklyn to their "jobs" in New Jersey. Malchikov was the enforcer.

Natasha, Vanessa, Liza, Lolita, and about thirty others were forced to work in northern New Jersey clubs six days a week under the menacing and brutal hand of the ex-boxer. Under his direction and others, the women were forced to dance naked and perform lap dances and other sexual favors for money.

"The trade generates thousands of dollars a week for dancers who are forced to kick in between $200 and $600 a day to the people who brought them here—money that over the years has attracted violence," wrote Zambito. He also pointed out that Veronica Chaschina, a twenty-eight-year-old Russian girl who fell into the same trap and worked against her will as a stripper, was murdered in April 2000. She was shot by an acquaintance who believed she was hiding more than $100,000 that she had earned as a sexual slave. No money was ever found, and it was unlikely one of these women would have been able to hide so much, given how their handlers scam them.

Of course, Trakhtenberg denied these allegations. He said he was forced into the business by local unnamed Russian mafia leaders. He insisted that his name was forged on all their documents, most likely by these women, who were just trying to get into the country illegally.

"I never smuggled anybody," Trakhtenberg told Zambito as he sipped Russian cognac in his apartment in Brooklyn, where he was under house arrest. He claims the women came to the U.S. voluntarily. He is awaiting trial in October 2004 in Newark Federal Court.

"The fearful plight of these women, who were forced to dance nude and perform other abhorrent acts, cannot be measured in a 12-count indictment. Their plight can only be measured in human tragedy," New Jersey Attorney General Peter Harvey told Zambito.

"These women are not doing this of their own

choice," Jersey City Police Lt. Walter Zalisko told a group gathered last month at the Ukrainian Institute of America on East 79th St. for the screening of a film that dramatized the problem. "They're slaves."

Zalisko told Zambito that he had interviewed more than 800 women in the New York and New Jersey region, who were forced to perform as dancers and/or prostitutes, some as young as fifteen years old.

"It's like a cancer that has gone undetected and has metastasized," said Rep. Chris Smith (R-N.J.), a sponsor of the Trafficking Victims Protection Act. As Zambito pointed out, "since 2001, the Justice Department has charged 149 traffickers - three times the number from the previous three years. Over the same period, 287 prosecutions were opened." However, this is only a small percentage of the actual women who are annually brought in and forced to endure such grotesque hardships.

LUDWIG "TARZAN" FAINBERG

Ludwig "Tarzan" Fainberg is a former Israeli mobster who, according to the FBI, acted as a broker for a series

of drug-and weapons-smuggling operations between
Colombian drug lords and the Russian Mafia in
Miami. Fainberg's exploits were legendary; the
eccentric Israeli once plotted to purchase a Soviet
submarine to transport cocaine from South America to
California, staying deep in the ocean to avoid
detection. The Soviet vessel would supposedly have had
its torpedo tubes packed with contraband and require a
crew of more than sixty men to operate. Ultimately, the
deal fell through for Fainberg, but it wasn't long before
he caught the attention of the FBI in the 1990s while he
was running Porky's, a strip club in Hialeah. The FBI
believed it was heavily involved in trafficking women
from the former Soviet Union.

In his book *The Natashas*, author Victor Malarek
describes an encounter with Feinberg, who bragged
about the ease of trafficking women from Russia, the
Ukraine, Romania, or the Czech Republic into the
United States. "No problem," he told Malarek. "The
price is $10,000 with the girl landed. It is simple. It is
easy to get access to the girls. It's a phone call. I know the
brokers in Moscow, St. Petersburg and Kyiv. I can call

Moscow tomorrow and show you how easy it is. I can get ten to fifteen to twenty girls shipped to me in a week."

In 1990, Fainberg began running Porky's, and by the end of the decade, he was convicted on racketeering charges and sentenced to just over three years in prison. But before his arrest, the man called "Tarzan" was under surveillance by the FBI and the United States's Drug Enforcement Agency. To their horror, agents watched one instance when Fainberg chased a stripper out of Porky's and proceeded to ram her head into a car door. On another occasion, agents saw Fainberg beat one dancer in the parking lot before forcing her to eat gravel. After serving his time in a U.S. prison, Fainberg relocated to Canada, where he was arrested again as a threat to public safety and ultimately deported to Israel.

Although Fainberg would deny that he was a trafficker as opposed to a businessman with dealings in trafficked women, there is no question that his industry provides a major source of income for crime rings around the world. They all operate with the same objectives, and they only vary in cultural or international dynamics. Asian traffickers, for example, pay smugglers between $10,000 and $15,000 for every successful female that is brought to the United States. This money will cover the cost of a passport on the black market (typically between $1,500 and $3,000), a one-way airline ticket, and additional fees. Thai smugglers, sometimes known as "jockeys," assist in bringing women into the United States for about $1,000 per journey, and recruitment agents receive a commission of approximately $1,000 for each woman recruited. This leaves a profit for the smuggler of about $7,500 to $9,000 per woman.

Over time, the profits from this trade can be significant. Thai traffickers who enslaved Thai men and women in a sweatshop in southern California are believed to have made more than $8 million over a six-year period. In New York, Thai traffickers who incarcerated and forced Thai women into a life of prostitution made more than $1.5 million in just over a year, charging their captives more than $30,000 each to pay their "debts." These women were forced to collect $130 from each client, with the madam of the brothel receiving $30 and the smugglers receiving the rest. Depending on the woman's beauty, the slave might also be sold outright to the madam for $15,000 or more. Similar enterprises around the world can be found in most major cities with Chinese and Malaysian sex slaves.

An organized task force in Atlanta indicted thirteen members of an Asian smuggling ring for trafficking more than 1,000 Asian women and girls between the ages of thirteen and twenty-five, for prostitution in Atlanta and other U.S. cities. The typical debt-slavery scenarios unfolded, with the girls forced to pay off thousands in "contract" debt, but some of the brothels where they worked were described by law enforcement officials as "prison compounds" with barbed wire, chained dogs, and gang members who worked around the brothel as guards.

The Coalition Against Trafficking Women reported that operators of the Hong Kong Spa in Washington, D.C., were running ads in international Asian newspapers for restaurant jobs that paid between $1,000 and $2,700 a week. When these teenage girls arrived, they were picked up at the airport and taken to brothels and massage parlors and forced to work fifteen-hour days. The trafficking of teenage girls appears to be a growing issue, according the Richards report for the CIA. In the mid-1990s, Mexican women—and girls—some as young as fourteen years old—were smuggled into the United States and forced to become prostitutes. The traffickers had promised to secure good jobs in landscaping, childcare, and elder care for the girls, and went to great lengths to assure the girls' parents that these jobs were legitimate.

CHUI PING CHENG, AKA "BIG SISTER PING"

In July 2003, the Bureau of Immigration and Customs Enforcement (ICE) successfully extradited Chui Ping Cheng, aka "Big Sister Ping," from Hong Kong to the United States after a long extradition battle. Cheng had been wanted by the ICE since 1994, when she was indicted by a New York grand jury for alien smuggling, kidnapping, hostage-taking, and money-laundering (also known as the "Snakehead" business). She was finally arrested in April 2000, after a five-year worldwide investigation by the ICE and the New York office of the FBI. Cheng appealed the extradition for three years in the Hong Kong courts until she exhausted all legal possibilities and was forced to comply.

Big Sister Ping smuggled thousands of Chinese migrants into the United States over a sixteen-year period ending in 2000, and it is believed she charged fees of up to $30,000 per person. "It may have taken ten years to get Cheng into a U.S. court for smuggling thousands of Chinese migrants, but that only demonstrates the ICE's resolve to identify, investigate, locate, and bring to prosecution those who traffic in human beings," said Michael J. Garcia, Acting Assistant Secretary for the ICE.

Cheng was the head of a sophisticated and far-reaching human trafficking ring and worked as a banker in Chinatown in New York City, operating a storefront on Broadway. Authorities believe she was using the storefront to launder her vast profits from the smuggling trade. In a news conference, deputy U.S. Attorney David Kelley stated, "It's really a case of an enterprising individual who took advantage of those so desperate to escape the poverty and misery of their homeland. But while promising passage to their dreams, Sister Ping often only delivered a nightmare and sometimes death."

The government is accusing Cheng of holding illegal immigrants in warehouses until their debts—typically in the range of $30,000—were paid. They were threatened with death and dismemberment if they did not pay their debts. The case came to light in June 1993, when a small ship named the Golden Venture ran aground off New York and ten Chinese immigrants drowned while attempting to swim to shore. In all, more than 300 people were packed into the dilapidated freighter, hoping to live the American dream.

According to a Congressional Research Service Report for Congress titled *Trafficking in Women and Children: The U.S. and International Response*, by Francis T. Miko, the trafficking in humans for prostitution and forced labor is one of the fastest-growing areas of international criminal activity. Overwhelmingly, it is women and children who are trafficked, and the Department of

State estimates that nearly one million humans are trafficked across borders each year on a worldwide basis. While Asia continues to have the most victims of human trafficking, the former Soviet Union and Eastern Europe are now believed to be the largest source of trafficking for prostitution and the sex industry in both Europe and North America.

U.S. law defines trafficking in persons as "sex trafficking in which a commercial sex act is induced by force, fraud, or coercion, or in which the person induced to perform such act has not attained eighteen years of age; or...the recruitment, harboring, transportation, provision, or obtaining of a person for labor or services, through the use of force, fraud, or coercion for the purpose of subjection to involuntary servitude, peonage, debt bondage, or slavery." Ludwig "Tarzan" Fainberg may not consider himself a human trafficker, but U.S. law clearly did.

The increase in human trafficking is directly attributable to criminal involvement, because it feeds on poverty, despair, war, and crisis. With the world economy moving toward more and more globalization, human movement between borders has increased both legally and illegally—most notably in the movement from poor to wealthier nations. Organized crime, on an international basis, has reacted to world business trends and has been able to exploit those at the lower end of the economic development scale. The collapse of Communism in the former Soviet Union has also caused severe economic hardships, expanding the black market for goods, services, and human labor. Another factor in the increase in human trafficking is the fact that prostitution is either legal or simply tolerated in many countries, and authorities are more inclined to go after the prostitutes themselves than to go after the traffickers. These conditions enable the Lekus, the Tarzans, and the Big Sister Pings of the world to thrive.

3.

History of Slavery

The Ancient and African Slave Trades

By definition, slavery is involuntary servitude which is enforced by violence, coercion, or other methods, which, according to the 1926 Slavery Convention, permit "the status or condition of a person over whom any or all of the powers attaching to the right of ownership are exercised." But while modern slavery is usually a variation of economically based debt slavery, ancient slavery often had its roots in punishment for crimes committed or as servitude for prisoners of war. From a historical perspective, those taken as slaves often were chosen because of their ethnicity, religion, race, or nationality, and slavery made great nations rich. There are prehistoric graves in Egypt that indicate that Libyans may have enslaved

Bushmen or Negrito people in 8000 B.C., and that Egyptian slave labor was used to build the great pyramids and temples.

In the ancient Mediterranean world, the majority of slaves were condemned to industrial or agricultural labor, and many of the great philosophers of the day viewed slavery as a natural order of things and a necessary institution for civil societies. The Greek philosopher Aristotle (384 B.C. – 322 B.C.) declared all barbarians to be slaves by birth, unable to rise beyond their obedient destinies. In his first book, Politics, he wrote, "Humanity is divided into two: the masters and the slaves; or, if one prefers it, the Greeks and the Barbarians, those who have the right to command, and those who are born to obey." He also wrote, "A slave is a property with a soul," and thus, slavery became an institution that would build empires.

Roman law stated that slaves had no head in the State, no name, no title, no register. They also had no rights of matrimony and no form of recourse against adultery, and they could be bought and sold or given away as personal property or even put to death at the owner's discretion. Roman ladies were instructed to punish their maids with sharp metal instruments for even the most mundane violations or improprieties. In contrast to the agricultural slave, urban slaves in ancient Greece and Rome were often given a chance at freedom, or manumission, at the will of their owners. Slaves could be rewarded for high productivity or loyal service. It was even possible for them to purchase their way out of servitude, but the process was by no means systematic or even logical. Slaves in Rome were usually organized into their own social class, and often the only property they were permitted to possess was the ability to reproduce. Men and women were exchanged like goods and services, and slaves had little hope for a better life.

There was, however, a class of freedmen and freedwomen who were known as *liberati* in Roman society. There was never an abundance of them, but Roman philosophy held that acts of kindness such as freeing slaves needed to be given in certain cases to demonstrate the great spirit of the civitas. Freed slaves, therefore, were celebrated as hopeful icons, often made famous as examples of a great society. Although they were not permitted to hold high office or marry into better classes, their children were usually granted the same rights as those of their fellow Roman citizens.

In ancient Egypt, slavery conditions were quite different from those in Greece and Rome. *Hem* (Hm) is generally translated as "slave," with the original meaning of "body," and hemu were either traded by slave merchants or were actual prisoners of war. It appears such Egyptian slaves were not relegated to a lifetime of servitude, but rather they became debt slaves and were sometimes given their freedom after a certain length of service. Slaves could be personal servants or the property of noblemen, estates, or temples, often as the result of a successful military campaign.

There is evidence that some Egyptians were sold into slavery to relinquish debts, or they may even have sold themselves to escape their own desolate living conditions. However, these indentured slaves did not necessarily give up all their rights after entering into servitude. During the New Kingdom, when pharaohs sought to conquer Syria, Canaan, and Nubia, a great many slaves were gained as prisoners of war and were brought back to Egypt. In the campaigns of Thutmose III, prisoners were taken and enslaved as a tribute from the defeated nation.

"The number of spoil taken in them . . . of vile Naharina who were as defenders among them, with their horses, 691 prisoners, 29 hands (of slain), 48 markes . . . in that year 295 male and female slaves, 68 horses, 3 gold dishes, 3 silver dishes, . . . "

Report from the forty-second year of the reign of Thutmose III W.M.F. Petrie *A History of Egypt* Part II p. 122

In fact, when the Egyptians conquered the Nubians, the taxes Egypt levied included slaves. Many of these slaves were put to work in copper and gold mines in Nubia and Sinai—work that was a death sentence for a great number of the enslaved, who perished from the deplorable conditions in the heat of the desert. Others were simply forced to join the army.

The most fortunate slaves were put to work for pharaohs, the royal family, or nobility, and were afforded better living conditions. Among those enslaved by the Egyptians were the Hebrews and Babylonians, some of whom worked in the Pharaoh's palace and the houses of nobility—such as Joseph of the famous colorful coat. Moses led Hebrew slaves out of Egypt into freedom.

In 1250 A.D., the Mamluks—Turks brought to Egypt as slaves—rose to power and ruled the country after Egypt gave them military training and positions of high power in the army and government. After seizing power in Egypt, the Mamluks went on to conquer nearby countries but ultimately lost their power when Turkey invaded Egypt.

ANCIENT GREEK SLAVES

Slave labor was viewed as an important element in the development and maintenance of the ancient Greek world. Male slaves were usually relegated to industrial and agricultural duties, while female slaves were assigned to domestic work, which included cooking, serving food, childcare, and the fetching of water. The wealthier the household, the better off the female slaves were, and their duties of servitude might have been more specialized, such as housekeeper, cook, or nurse. Slaves in ancient Greece were owned by their employers, so there was a great deal of deviation in their treatment, depending on either their status within their owners' households, or the actual temperament of their owners. Because males and females were segregated in terms of their roles in ancient Greece, slave women were at an even greater disadvantage in society, not only because of their gender but because of the acceptance of the idea of male superiority in Greek culture. Female slaves often had to face sexual exploitation as well as physical abuse, and children born of master/slave relations had to be disposed of because female slaves were not permitted to raise children.

However, there is evidence that slave girls developed close relationships with their mistresses, and since these upper-class Greek women were often relegated to the private world of their own homes, many of them confided in their slaves out of the need for human interaction. Euripedes's tragic character Medea confided her innermost secrets to her nurse—a slave who both gave Medea advice and comforted her in times of trouble. It was not uncommon for slaves to accompany their mistresses anytime they left their houses.

ISLAMIC SLAVERY

Under the laws of Islam, slavery was permitted in the Islam and Arab worlds until the mid-twentieth century, and it was actually encouraged, though not required. Regarding manumission, it was forbidden to give slaves their freedom unless they wanted to be free. This "system" was actually designed to protect slaves and prevent them from going hungry during desolate times or when a slave was sick or hungry. Most of the slaves in Islamic culture were either the children of slaves or prisoners of war. But there was also the practice of *devsirme*, which was akin to debt slavery, where humans were acquired as payment of taxes.

Slaves in the Islamic world were also more

specialized, and aside from agricultural work, slaves could provide other forms of service as artisans, janissaries, concubines, and even eunuchs. For this reason, it was popular for the children of the wealthy to be skilled in some type of textilework, carpet-making, or gardening, should political tides turn. Should these children ever be captured and enslaved, the fact that they had certain skills would give them more value and perhaps save them from certain death. For roughly a thousand years, the Islamic world purchased and captured slaves from Africa and Europe, but race was not a factor in Arabian slavery under Islamic rule. In fact, the rise of Islam was widely viewed as a liberating force for those who were racially enslaved.

ANCIENT ROME

In the early years of the Roman Republic, most Romans owned and operated small farms, but the Punic Wars changed Roman society dramatically. Slaves were being brought into the republic (509 B.C. – 27 B.C.) in great numbers, where they were put to work on farms, making it possible for large plantations to prosper in the new slave-based republic. These slaves were the muscle that ultimately built the Roman Empire (27 B.C. − 476 A.D.), but generations later, slaves were also responsible for its downfall. At times during the empire, slaves often outnumbered freemen by three to one. Roman laws in place at the time offered few civil rights, slaves were infuriated by their brutal treatment, and revolts were not uncommon. The most famous revolt was led in 73-74 B.C. by Spartacus, whose army of slaves numbered close to 100,000 and was able to defeat two Roman armies before he was killed. The revolt centered in Campania in southern Italy, and many of those who revolted were agricultural and pastoral slaves. Thousands of Spartacus's soldiers were eventually captured and crucified.

Before Spartacus, a slave named Salvius led slaves to revolt in eastern Sicily while Athenion headed a movement by western slaves. It took Rome four years to put down the revolt, which lasted from 104-100 B.C. But the first slave revolt of the Roman Empire was led by a freeborn slave named Eunus who was from Syria. Eunus was believed to be a magician, and together with

Kleon, another slave manager who was reputed to possess mystical and religious powers, the two were able to gather slave troops and revolt against the Empire in 135-132 B.C. Eventually, the senate was able to send the Roman army out to decimate the rebellious slaves and ultimately put an end to the first slave war.

GLADIATORS

The rise in popularity of the gladiator was made possible by the many conquests of the Roman armies. Captured soldiers were often "recruited" during the imperial expansion of Rome. Vespasian and Titus eliminated an extraordinary number of rebellious Jews by putting gladiatorial contests in place after the pacification of Judea. Roman society also had the jurisdiction to sentence convicted criminals to gladiator-training schools, and owners of slaves were empowered to sell their slaves into the gladiatorial life.

While there was no question the life of a Roman gladiator was brutal, it is interesting to note that there were a number of citizens who chose the gladiatorial life for the economic security the "profession" provided. Gladiators were given three square meals each day and had access to decent medical care. If they were highly skilled, gladiators could be awarded freedom, and they would often make significant financial gains from contests in the form of purses as performance bonuses. Therefore, it was not uncommon for Roman citizens of a higher social status who were facing some kind of economically difficult times to enroll in a gladiator school.

The Romans were strong in the conviction that their gladiatorial games were inherited from the Etruscans, who the Romans believed used the contests as a funeral ritual, where servants or slaves would fight to the death for the honor of accompanying their owners or masters into the afterlife. There does not seem to be any evidence that the Etruscans actually held gladiatorial contests in such a way, but evidence does exist that the Campanian society did have gladiators. Tertullian wrote that "men believed that the souls of the dead were propitiated by human blood, so at funerals they sacrificed prisoners of war or slaves of poor quality for the purpose."

Junius Brutus Pera's sons are believed to have authorized Rome's first gladiatorial games in 265 B.C. to honor their father after his death, and these competitions quickly gained a popular following in Rome. Titus Flamininus sponsored more than seventy contests in honor of his fallen father in a spectacle that lasted more than three days, and Julius Caesar promised to put on more than three hundred matches in funeral games for his daughter, Julia. However, the senate voted to limit the amount of money that could be used for gladiatorial games, putting a stop to Caesar's wishes.

Later, Augustus allowed gladiatorial games to occur on a more frequent basis. With less of a funereal theme, gladiator contests, from a Roman point of view, were about the socially dead (prisoners of war, criminals, and slaves) and their battle for life and death. Gladiators, in their epic battles, were often given a chance for redemption if they displayed bravery and valor in their contests, win or lose. If they performed well, the crowd might be won over and demand that a defeated warrior be spared. Popular and victorious gladiators might inspire the Roman crowd to urge emperors to free these bravest of warriors.

As a society, the Romans faced mortality rates that forced the young to contemplate death at an early age. It was rare for young men to live longer than thirty years, and gladiators provided examples for these men to observe in regard to facing death with dignity and courage. It is also apparent that the Romans valued the skills associated with killing in hand-to-hand combat, since the empire was built by citizens and soldiers conquering many lands in such manner. Gladiators epitomized these battles and provided metaphorical examples of many of the ideals that the Romans held dear to them.

The gladiatorial games enabled Rome to put on display the power of the Roman Empire, since producing these games was incredibly expensive. They became so popular that they began to spread across the empire, and the staged battles became big business for entrepreneurs. Wild animals were often captured from around the world and brought back to Rome to be displayed in newly built stadiums. There were gladiators who specialized in combat against animals, and these battles coincided with the Roman fixation on the most basic contrasts between life and death. Wild animals were considered formidable forces of nature that man had to contend with and overcome for his survival. Lions and tigers were often pitted against slaves, Christians, and gladiators as either a form of punishment or in simple battles to the death for the sake of spectacle. These battles often symbolized a civilized society and its attempt to protect itself from the most hostile forces nature had to offer. Other times, the gladiators were seen as symbols of the outlaw—the barbarians in the world who were a constant threat to civilized society.

A Gladiatorial show is apt to seem cruel and brutal to some eyes, and I incline to think that it is so, as now conducted. But in the days when it was criminals who crossed swords in the death struggle, there could be no better schooling against pain and death. —Cicero, Tusculans

There were some who felt that gladiator battles were provided to the Roman masses as a diversion—to maintain the peace in the empire. Gladiators trained in ways similar to the way that professional athletes train today. They were schooled in the use of various weapons, such as the net, trident, dagger, and war chain, as well as swords and defensive shields. They did not, however, wear the armor of the Roman military, as this might send the wrong message to the populace in attendance. Rather, they wore the armor and used the weaponry of non-Romans—generally from lands that Rome had conquered. For example, a gladiator might dress as a Samnite, sporting a large oblong shield (also known as a *scutum*), a visored helmet, and a sword (*gladius*). Other roles gladiators might play were those of the Thracian, the Secutor or the Retiarius.

Despite their often lowly status, gladiators were usually paid every time they battled. If a gladiator managed to survive for three to five years, he was often given his freedom. But these types of gladiator heroes were rare. If an opponent was hurt in battle, the crowd might shout, *"Habet, hoc habet"* (he's had it!), and then he might raise his left hand with a finger extended, asking for mercy. There would then be a vote for life or death for the defeated gladiator. If the decision was for death, the conquering gladiator would thrust his sword through the loser's neck. Then two attendants usually dressed as Charon and Mercury would remove the body of the defeated gladiator, and the winner would receive a token for his victory, such as a gold coin or bowl. Despite their low social standing and outlaw status, gladiators often attracted Roman matrons who wanted to have affairs with them, and young Roman boys were infatuated with gladiator schools and were sometimes given fighting lessons by their gladiator heroes.

SLAVERY AFTER THE FALL OF ROME

By the fifth century, the Roman Empire had fallen, yet slavery—instrumental in the success of the empire, did not die. In fact, slavery simply morphed into serfdom—part of the feudal economy, where labor was no longer the property of an owner, but instead was bound to the land. From England to Wales to Eastern Europe, slaves existed in society as far back as the early Middle Ages. Interestingly enough, many of the slave-trade routes that are used today follow the same slave routes of the Middle Ages and the Renaissance, as Slavic women and children were bought and sold to Western Europe. During the Middle Ages, thousands of women and children from Poland, the Czech lands, Latvia, East Prussia, and Estonia were taken to Italy and southern France to serve as slaves for more "cultured" societies. Later, it was Russian and Ukrainian women, along with Bosnians and Albanians, who were trafficked into Italy and the Middle East. Ultimately, the Ottoman Empire conquered Constantinople, effectively putting an end to the Eastern European slave market.

Throughout the Middle Ages, Mediterranean piracy by the Muslims of Spain seized Christians and brought them home from the high seas to a life of slavery. Moorish Spain trafficked slaves on such a large scale that there were, at times, German, Russian, Slav, Greek, Sudanese, Nubian, and Ethiopian slaves to be seen and purchased in the Muslim markets. On a smaller scale, Vikings plundered villages all across Europe, returning to Scandinavia with slaves who

helped establish a caste system of their own. But after
the Middle Ages, a new slave trade was in the making.
The Atlantic slave trade would take more than eleven
million black slaves from Africa to the Americas,
encompassing one of the most elaborate and profitable
commercial slavery ventures the world had ever known.

AFRICAN SLAVERY

The African slave trade peaked in the late 1700s when
slaves were captured in West Africa and shipped to the
New World in larger waves than ever to meet demand.
Some estimate that over the centuries, more than
twelve million Africans were taken and up to fifteen
percent did not survive the journey. The overwhelming
majority of these slaves ended up in the Americas, but
Europe and South Africa also claimed their fair share
of forced labor. The following is a timeline that
represents the earliest known practices of what would
eventually become a massive industry that endured for
centuries.

AFRICAN SLAVERY TIMELINE

1441   Presumed to signal the beginning of slave abduction in Africa, Antao Goncalves and Nuno Tristao, Portuguese explorers, take twelve Africans in Cabo Branco and bring them to Portugal as slaves.

1444   A tax collector from the Portuguese town of Lagos named Lancarote de Freitas sets up a company to trade with Africa, and brings 235 kidnapped and enslaved Africans to Lagos. This was presumed to be the largest group to date of Africans taken to Europe for a life of slavery.

1452   Sugar is first planted on Madeira, a Portuguese island, and African slaves begin what becomes a long history of work on sugar plantations.

1452   Pope Nicholas V issues Dum Diversas, which authorizes the Portuguese to reduce non-Christians to the status of slaves.

1454   Pope Nicholas V grants the Portuguese a slave-trading monopoly with Africa with his Romanus Pontifex, yet Spanish traders begin trading in slaves from Africa.

1461   The castle of Arguin, the first of the Portuguese trading forts, is completed.

1462   Portuguese slave traders begin operations in Seville (Spain).

1470   In spite of opposition from the Pope, Spanish merchants begin engaging in the trafficking of slaves.

1476	Carlos de Valera of Castille in Spain returns with four hundred slaves from Africa.
1479	Spain and Portugal sign the Treaty of Alacovas, which gives Portugal the right to supply Spain with all the African slaves it needs.
1481	A Portuguese embassy to the court of King Edward IV of England agrees with the English government's decision not to enter the slave trade—a decision that angered many English traders.
1481-86	The castle at Elmina (modern Ghana) is built by Diogo da Azambuja. It would become the most notorious of all the slave-trading forts in West Africa.
1486	The Portuguese settle the West African island of Sao Tome, planting sugar and using African slaves to develop the plantations.
1488	Christopher Columbus is greeted in El Mina Forgress by Africans in Ghana, West Africa.
1492	The Moorish town of Granada surrenders to the Spanish forces of the Catholic Kings, Ferdinand and Isabella, which marks the end of La Reconquista, the war between the Spaniards and the Moors.
1492	Christopher Columbus discovers the New World, landing in the Bahamas. Pedro Alonzo Nina, a black man, arrives with Columbus.
1493	Columbus returns on his second voyage, this time landing in Dominica. He takes with him a shipment of hundreds of Taino people as slaves.

1496	Columbus brings about thirty Native American slaves back to Italy.
1497	John Cabot, an Italian sponsored by King Henry VII of England, lands on the northern tip of Newfoundland, the basis for English claims to all of North America.
1500	Pedro Cabral of Portugal discovers Brazil, landing at Porto Seguro.
1502	The first reported African slaves are taken to the New World by Juan de Cordoba, a merchant of Seville, Spain.
1504	A small group of African slaves captured from a Portuguese vessel are taken before the court of King James IV of Scotland.
1505	Sugarcane is grown in Santa Domingo, marking the first sugar crop grown in the New World.
1510	Believed to be the beginning of the systematic transportation of African slaves to the New World, King Ferdinand of Spain approves a shipment of fifty African slaves to Santo Domingo.
1513	Juan Ponce de Leon becomes the first European to reach the coast of what is now Florida in the United States.
1513	Spain authorizes the use of African slaves in Cuba, and thirty black men accompany Balboa when he discovers the Pacific Ocean.
1516	Diego Velazques, the governor of Cuba, authorizes slave-raiding expeditions to Central America. One such group of slaves aboard a Spanish vessel rebels and kills the Spanish crew before sailing home. This was believed to be the first successful slave rebellion recorded in the New World.

1518	Charles V grants his Flemish courtier Lorenzo de Gorrevod permission to import four thousand African slaves into New Spain, marking the beginning of an escalation in the slave trade to the New World.
1522	A large slave rebellion takes place on the island of Hispaniola—the first of many uprisings that would become common occurrences.
1524	Three hundred African slaves are brought to Cuba to work in gold mines.
1526	Heinrich Eninger and Hieronymous Seiler of Konstanz become the first known Germans to get involved in the slave trade.
1527	The production of sugar in the Caribbean increases dramatically, with African slaves providing almost all the labor.
1528	Esteban (or Estevanico) becomes the first African slave to reach what is now the Continental United States. He is one of only four survivors of Panfilo de Narvaez's failed expedition to Florida.
1532	William Hawkins of Plymouth becomes the first English mariner to arrive on the coast of West Africa. He does not participate in slave trading, however.
1539	Following reports from Cabeza de Vaca, Hernando de Soto lands on the coast of Florida. Of about one thousand two hundred men in his expedition, about fifty were African slaves.
1555	Portuguese sailor Fernao de Oliveira denounces the slave trade as an "evil trade" in his book, Arte de Guerra no Mar (The Art of War at Sea).

1555   Under pressure from the Spanish rulers, Queen Mary of England forbids English involvement in Guinea.

1556   Genoa, Italy, makes an attempt to prevent slave trade, not for humanitarian reasons, but to reduce the number of Africans in the city.

1556   In his work, *De justicia et de jure libri X (Ten books on Justice and Law)*, Domingo de Soto makes the argument that it is wrong to enslave any person who was born free.

1562   John Hawkins of Plymouth becomes the first known English sailor to obtain African slaves when he takes three hundred from Sierra Leone to sell in the West Indies. Hawkins traded the slaves illegally with Spanish colonies at a great profit and returned on later trips for more business, creating tensions between England and Spain. (Hawkins not only introduced the slave trade to England, but he brought tobacco and potatoes as well.)

1571   The Parlement of Bordeaux sets all slaves (including blacks and moors) free, declaring slavery in France illegal.

1580   After the death of King Henry of Portugal and a short campaign by the Duke of Alva, Spain and Portugal are united under Phillip II of Spain. Spain becomes the most important colonial power and the largest participant in the slave trade.

1585   Sir Walter Raleigh organizes the first English colony in the New World at Roanoke Island (now North Carolina), but the settlers fail and the colonists withdraw the following year.

1585	Sir Francis Drake attacks Santiago's slave-trading settlement in the Cape Verde Islands, and begins a series of attacks that contribute to the war between England and Spain.
1587	Walter Raleigh once again organizes a colony at Roanoke Island, and when English ships return to the settlement three years later, the colony is nowhere to be found.
1592	Bernard Ericks becomes the first Dutch slave trader.
1595	Philip II of Spain grants Pedro Gomes Reinal from Portugal a virtual monopoly in the slave trade. Reinal agrees to a deal with Spanish America to provide more than four thousand African slaves on an annual basis. This agreement would last for decades, well after Reinal's death in 1600.
1601	Jesuits build the first sugar mill in Brazil.
1607	The first permanent British colony in North America is founded in Jamestown, Virginia.
1617	First recorded notations of slaves arriving in Bermuda.
1640	The beginning of large-scale trafficking of African slave labor in the British Caribbean for sugar production.
1755	Olaudah Equiano is born in Nigeria and later sold into slavery. Equiano would later publish his autobiography (*The Interesting Narrative of the Live of Olaudah Equiano*, 1789) and become a leading voice in the anti-slavery movement.

1791	The Haitian Revolution begins as a slave uprising near Le Cap in the French West Indian colony of Santo Domingo and leads to the establishment of the black nation of Haiti in 1801.
1793	White refugees begin pouring into ports of the United States, fleeing the insurrection in Santo Domingo.
1794	All slaves in the French colonies are emancipated in the French National Convention.
1794	The U.S. Congress passes legislation that prohibits the manufacture, fitting, equipping, loading, or dispatching of any vessel to be employed in the slave trade.
1794	Eli Whitney patents his cotton gin device for pulling seeds from cotton. The invention turns cotton into the cash crop of the American South—and creates a great demand for slave labor.
1795	Pinckney's Treaty establishes commercial relations between the United States and Spain.
1800	The United States enacts strong penalties for American citizens who serve voluntarily in slave trading between nations.
1804	The Republic of Haiti is proclaimed.
1807	The British Parliament bans participation in the Atlantic slave trade.
1807	The United States passes legislation banning slave trade, effective in 1808. But slave smuggling continues.

1810	Britain negotiates an agreement with Portugal, which calls for the gradual abolition of slave trading in the South Atlantic.
1815	At the Congress of Vienna, the British put pressure on Spain, Portugal, France, and the Netherlands to agree to abolish the slave trade (though Spain and Portugal are permitted to trade slaves for labor replenishment reasons for a few years afterward).
1817	Spain and Great Britain sign a treaty prohibiting the slave trade. Spain agrees to end the slave trade north of the equator immediately, and south of the equator in 1820. British naval vessels are given the right to search suspected slave ships.
1819	Spain and the United States renew commercial agreements in the Adams-Oris Treaty. The U.S. Congress also passes legislation stiffening provisions against American involvement in the slave trade.
1820	Missouri is admitted to the Union as a slave state, and Maine as a free state. Slavery is forbidden in any subsequent territories north of latitude 360 30', known as the Missouri Compromise.
1822	Denmark Vesey, a freed slave in South Carolina, attempts a rebellion in Charleston, and thirty-five participants are hanged in the ill-fated uprising.
1824	The United States and Great Britain negotiate a treaty that recognizes the slave trade as piracy and establish procedures for joint suppression. However, the Senate undercuts the treaty's power in a series of amendments, and Britain refuses to sign.

1825	A U.S. Revenue cutter seizes the Antelope, a ship sailing under a Venezuelan flag with a cargo of two hundred eighty-one Africans. The case reaches the U.S. Supreme Court, which issues a unanimous opinion declaring that the slave trade is a violation of natural law. However, Africans destined for Spain, Portugal, and Venezuela are not set free, since the law had no authority over those nations.
1831	A large slave revolt breaks out in Jamaica, and is brutally repressed. That same year, Nat Turner, a Virginia slave preacher, leads a two-day uprising against whites, killing sixty. Militiamen crush the revolt and ultimately hang Turner. This leads to harsher restrictions against slaves.
1833	Great Britain passes the Abolition of Slavery Act, which provides for emancipation in the British West Indies—to take effect in 1834.
1835	The Anglo-Spanish agreement on the slave trade is renewed, and enforcement is tightened. This same year sees southern U.S. states expel abolitionists and forbid the mailing of antislavery propaganda.
1837	Britain requests that the United States and France create an international patrol to interdict slaving. The United States declines.
1849	After fleeing slavery herself, Harriet Tubman returns to the South more than fifteen times to help rescue hundreds of slaves.
1854	The Missouri Compromise is set aside in the Kansas-Nebraska Act, which Congress passed to allow these two new territories to choose whether to allow slavery. The act leads to violent clashes.

1857   The United States Supreme Court decides that blacks can
        never be citizens and that Congress has no authority to
        outlaw slavery in any territory.

1860   Abraham Lincoln of Illinois is elected to the office of
        President of the United States.

1860   South Carolina secedes in December, and more states
        follow the next year.

1861-65 The United States Civil War claims 623,000 lives.

1863   Abraham Lincoln decrees that all slaves in Rebel territory
        are free on January 1, 1863.

1865   The Thirteenth Amendment to the United States
        Constitution outlaws slavery.

This timeline was compiled from numerous sources, including
The Mystic Seaport Museum (Exploring Amistad),
Africanaonline.com, and brycchancarey.com.

4.

Breaking the New Slave Trade

Global Trafficking Hot Spots

"Not only here in the United States, but around the world, so that people understand the horrible nature of this crime, and that they don't just view it as a cultural artifact or a way of someone looking for a better life and maybe being mistreated, but no harm done. They've got to understand that this is really at root a criminal enterprise that crosses all boundaries," U.S. Senator Hillary Rodham Clinton told Jamie Rubin of PBS Wide Angle, "Dying to Leave" (9/25/03).

Each year, the U.S. Department of State issues its annual Trafficking in Persons Report to highlight the international crisis of human trafficking and to identify each country's laws, policies, and practices. The 2003 report is the most comprehensive worldwide report on the efforts of governments to combat severe forms of trafficking in persons. The annual trafficking report includes those countries that have a significant number of victims of severe forms of trafficking. The narratives provide an overview of the trafficking situation in the country and the U.S. government's efforts to combat trafficking.

The following are selected passages from the 2003 Trafficking in Persons Report with an emphasis on "Global Hot Spots in Human Trafficking." Countries have been ranked by the U.S. Department of State into three "tiers," as defined below.

THE TIERS

Tier 1: Countries whose governments fully comply with the Act's minimum standards.

Tier 2: Countries whose governments do not fully comply with the Act's minimum standards but are making significant efforts to bring themselves into compliance with those standards.

Tier 3: Countries whose governments do not fully comply with the minimum standards and are not making significant efforts to do so.

In this report, for the first time, governments that are not making significant efforts to bring themselves into compliance with the minimum standards—those listed on Tier 3—face potential sanctions that include loss of certain types of U.S. assistance.

TURKEY

Turkey, which is classified as Tier 3—a hotbed of slavery—is a destination country for persons trafficked for the purposes of sexual exploitation and labor. It is also a country of transit to other European destinations for women and girls trafficked for sexual exploitation. Most of these victims come from countries of the former Soviet Union, including Azerbaijan, Georgia, Armenia, Russia, Ukraine, and Moldova.

The Government of Turkey does not fully comply with the minimum standards for the elimination of trafficking, and it is not making significant efforts to do so. Overall, the government is to be commended for its new antitrafficking criminal article and the law enforcement efforts, including strengthening immigration laws, which were made recently. However, the government's progress was slow in the past year, particularly in the areas of prevention and protection—namely, deportation without screenings—and those areas need significant improvement.

The Turkish government did not implement any trafficking-specific preventive campaigns, but it evidenced some increased political will to address the trafficking issue. The Ministry of Foreign Affairs chairs an interagency task force on trafficking. The task force does not meet regularly, but it has drafted a national action plan that the government adopted in April 2003. The government amended its laws to allow a centralized system of work permits for foreign nationals entering Turkey under legitimate programs. The new law authorizes foreigners to work as domestics, a practice that was once illegal. The government actively monitors its borders, but they are long and porous and difficult to monitor in some regions. Turkey's cooperation with countries that are sources of trafficking was reportedly limited, although improvement efforts were initiated in the spring of 2003.

The Turkish government amended its criminal code in the past year to prohibit trafficking in persons (Article 201/b). The law prescribes serious penalties that are increased with aggravating circumstances. As of April 2003, six trafficking cases were opened in Turkish penal courts pursuant to the new article, against a total of seventeen suspects. In two cases, the court ruled for acquittal, finding three defendants not guilty and determining that the two alleged victims had not been illegally trafficked. The other four cases are ongoing. In these cases, fourteen suspects will be on trial and twelve people have filed complaints against them. More trafficking-related arrests were made in the past year and referred to the courts, but no convictions were reported under previously existing laws. The Ministries of Justice and Interior conducted training on the antitrafficking legislation.

The government does not have a system for victim

identification and protection; however, according to the Ministry of Interior, seven foreign citizens exposed to trafficking were issued a humanitarian visa (a one-month temporary residence permit). Five additional people were offered the humanitarian visa but declined and requested to leave Turkey. The government supports shelters for Turkish victims of domestic violence and while it claims those shelters can be used to serve trafficking victims, they have not yet been reported to do so. Some local law enforcement officers reportedly find accommodation for victims, and pay for it out of their personal expenses. Turkey's cooperation with countries that are sources of trafficking was reportedly ineffective, and the government continued to deport potential victims as criminals without consistently exploring their true nationality and without screening them properly as victims. The Turkish government does not have a repatriation program, and its discussions with the International Organization for Migration were unsuccessful.

UZBEKISTAN

Uzbekistan is primarily a source, and to a lesser extent, a transit country for the purposes of prostitution and labor. It is classified as a Tier 3 country. Confirmed information on the extent of trafficking from Uzbekistan only recently emerged, and there is a concern that the deterioration in the country's economy may lead to a growing problem with trafficking. Known destinations are Kazakhstan, United Arab Emirates, South Korea, Malaysia, Thailand, Kosovo, and Israel. According to economists, 40-80 percent of the population has fallen into poverty in the eleven years since Uzbekistan's independence from the Soviet Union. Many of these newly poor earn less than one dollar per day.

The government of Uzbekistan does not fully comply with the minimum standards for the elimination of trafficking, and it is not making significant efforts to do so. The government of Uzbekistan only recently recognized that it has a problem with trafficking in persons, and that trafficking could become a greater problem if left unchecked. During the spring of 2003, central government authorities showed a greater willingness to focus on the issue, especially through improved dialogue with victim-assistance nongovernmental organizations. This recognition came late in the reporting period, and now Uzbekistan's treatment of known victims and of women fitting the victim profile must be improved.

The government has thus far taken only limited preventive actions of its own. The government denies exit from Uzbekistan to young women, does not screen them to determine if they are victims, and does not offer them preventive information on trafficking. The government worked alongside other organizations on prevention in some instances, such as the permission granted by the Ministry of Education to one nongovernmental organization to conduct antitrafficking programs in schools. Some regions have been more proactive than the central government, with the regional government's Women's Committee in Samarkand engaging with nongovernmental organizations to establish information-sharing and referral for victims.

The criminal code of Uzbekistan does not contain antitrafficking laws. Other criminal articles prohibit various aspects of trafficking in persons, and the government pursued some criminal investigations under these laws, but there have been no final prosecutions or convictions of traffickers in Uzbekistan. An organized trafficking ring from Uzbekistan to Kazakhstan was exposed in February 2003. Under international pressure, the government investigated this case and has expelled two North Koreans who were responsible. However, the Prosecutor General has taken actions against illegal recruitment, especially through marriage agencies and tourist firms, and is pursuing a case involving fifty-six men who may have been trafficking victims for labor in Siberia. It is also investigating the case of a girl trafficked for sex to the United Arab Emirates. Border guards reportedly harass returning victims and require payoffs at the border for women who possibly fit the victim profile. While no actions against this corruption were reported for the period covered by this report, in early 2002 the government convicted two border guards on corruption charges for allowing people to be trafficked.

The government of Uzbekistan does not have a mechanism for screening, recognizing, sheltering, or otherwise assisting victims, nor does it have a referral mechanism to victim-assistance nongovernmental organizations. However, it is increasing its efforts at victim assistance and protection. In late spring 2003, the government began to share information with one victim-assistance nongovernmental organization, and border officials informally agreed to provide that nongovernmental organization with greater access to returning victims at the airport. However, victims complain of harsh treatment by police and border agents upon their return. The government continued to charge a $25 fee to victims abroad who were seeking new travel documents. Most victims were not able to pay this fee. Nongovernmental organizations were unable to secure effective assistance from consular officers in many cases throughout the year. But, in the spring of 2003, the government began to respond to some of the pleas of nongovernmental organizations advocating for and assisting in the repatriation of victims, and it began using temporary travel documents to bring trafficking victims home from abroad. The government engaged in discussions with the International Organization for Migration regarding a repatriation program but still has not entered into any agreement for such a project.

KAZAKHSTAN

Kazakhstan, a former member of the Soviet Union, is a source, transit, and destination country for women and men who are trafficked for the purpose of sexual exploitation and labor. Victims are trafficked to and through Kazakhstan from the Kyrgyz Republic, Tajikistan, and Uzbekistan, and are trafficked from Kazakhstan to the United Arab Emirates, Greece, Cyprus, France, Italy, Portugal, Switzerland, Belgium, South Korea, Turkey, Israel, and Albania. Some internal trafficking has also been reported from rural areas to the cities.

The government of Kazakhstan is recognized as a Tier 3 offender and does not fully comply with the minimum standards for the elimination of trafficking. It is not making significant efforts to do so. The government's antitrafficking focus and activity dropped significantly last year, and it failed to follow through on plans devised in the previous year. However, it presented to Parliament a long-awaited draft of antitrafficking legislation, which passed the lower house of Parliament on May 15.

The Kazakhstan government's antitrafficking prevention was limited to campaigns conducted in varying degrees at the regional level. With the departure of the former head of the President's Commission on Women and Family from the position of government antitrafficking coordinator, the commission's focus on trafficking weakened. However, the commission, in conjunction with the Gender Crimes Unit of the Ministry of Interior, conducted research on trafficking victimization, although the results were not yet released by April 2003. Representatives of the commission conducted various preventive activities, such as circulating NGO-produced antitrafficking information in schools, in all 16 of Kazakhstan's administrative districts. The government began implementing a bilateral labor agreement with the Kyrgyz Republic that allows a quota of legally protected Kyrgyz workers to enter Kazakhstan.

The operative antitrafficking article in Kazakhstan, Article 330, criminalizes the organization of illicit migration, which includes trafficking across international borders and trafficking of minors. Some trafficking cases may be prosecuted under related crimes, such as recruitment for sexual or other exploitation and organization of brothels. While there were many reported investigations, officials reported no cases for any of the above-mentioned crimes that had proceeded to court. The police currently are investigating a case against a North Korean accused of trafficking women from Uzbekistan to Kazakhstan, as well as cases in Akmolinsk, northern Kazakhstan, southern Kazakhstan, and Zhambul oblasts. The government also cooperated with the governments of South Korea, the United Arab Emirates, and Turkey on trafficking cases. The Financial Police arrested the owner of a suspect travel agency after Almaty police dropped a criminal case against the same company. The civil case has been ongoing for two years, as have advocates' attempts to seek prosecution. The suspect is now in custody. A working group led by the Ministry of Justice completed a set of antitrafficking amendments to the criminal code and forwarded them to Parliament for a vote on May 15, 2004. The government appointed the Prosecutor General to take the lead as the focal point for trafficking efforts, and the Law Enforcement Coordinating Council is also working on antitrafficking strategies. The government has included a three-hour antitrafficking training module in the prosecutors' mandatory recertification training program.

The Kazakhstan government does not have a system for identifying potential victims among vulnerable groups, which puts possible victims at risk for summary deportation and criminalization during police street sweeps. The government provides some protection in individual cases that are brought to its attention, but it does not actively screen for victims in order to offer protection. The criminal procedure code allows for certain protections in and out of court for witnesses; however, lack of resources prevents protection for witnesses in trafficking cases. Government officials refer victims to nongovernmental organizations for services at the local level, although no reports were provided regarding actual victims assisted during the reporting period.

VIETNAM

Vietnam is a source, transit, and, to a lesser extent, destination country for persons trafficked for forced labor and sexual exploitation. Vietnamese women and girls are trafficked to Cambodia, Malaysia, China, Hong Kong, Macau, and Taiwan for sexual exploitation and forced marriages. Victims from China transit Vietnam on trafficking routes to Australia, Europe, and North America. Cambodian children are trafficked into Vietnam to beg in urban areas and give the money to their traffickers. Vietnamese rural laborers are exploited by traffickers. Labor export companies recruit and send workers abroad; some of these laborers have been known to suffer trafficking abuses.

The government of Vietnam does not fully comply with the minimum standards for the elimination of trafficking; however, it is making significant efforts to do so. Particular concern remains, however, about the government's effectiveness in addressing cases of labor exploitation. Vietnamese state-owned labor companies have entered into international contracts that have resulted in incidents of labor trafficking. The government needs to protect workers through better oversight measures in these companies, which it is supposed to regulate. Vietnam's efforts to combat trafficking for sexual exploitation could be enhanced by cooperating with Cambodia to address cross-border issues, including how to repatriate and care for victims of trafficking.

The government partners with multiple international organizations on antitrafficking studies and surveys, and takes limited prevention measures in at-risk communities through leaflets and community trainers. The government-controlled Vietnam

Women's Union sponsored an antitrafficking mass media campaign using television and newspapers. In other measures not specific to trafficking, the government is providing limited funds for development projects to increase compulsory education to nine years, and vocational and micro-credit programs for at-risk women and youth.

Although an inter-ministerial working group chaired by the deputy prime minister coordinates anti-sex trafficking activities, clarification of responsibility at the agency level is needed to focus government action. Vietnamese law includes a statute that prohibits sexual exploitation and the trafficking of women and children. The government investigates, arrests, and convicts sex traffickers; however, it does not make comprehensive statistics on arrests and convictions available, so the government's efforts cannot be fully evaluated. General statistics on trafficking in persons are not kept, but a much-needed proposed project would create a data-collection system within a new crime statistics office. The government has taken part in bilateral police cooperation to combat trafficking, sending officials to Cambodia and China for better information-sharing.

The Vietnamese government is also addressing corruption. High-profile efforts include bringing four trafficking cases to trial against local government officials in 2002, as well as one high-profile 2003 case, in which more than one hundred and fifty people, including ex-ministerial and ex-law enforcement officials, were indicted for prostitution and migrant-smuggling.

The government should take additional steps to ensure that recovering victims are not abused. Many women found engaged in prostitution are not jailed or given criminal records, but placed in one of more than forty rehabilitation centers. These centers reportedly provide medical treatment, vocational training, and counseling in an effort to discourage the victims from returning to prostitution.

PAKISTAN

Pakistan, a Tier 2 country, is a country of origin, transit, and destination for women and children trafficked for purposes of sexual exploitation and bonded labor. Internal trafficking of women and girls from rural areas to cities for the purpose of sexual exploitation and labor also occurs. Pakistan is a source country for young boys who are trafficked to the United Arab Emirates, Kuwait, and Qatar as camel jockeys. It is also a destination for women and children trafficked from Bangladesh, Afghanistan, Iran, and Central Asia for the purpose of commercial sexual exploitation and labor. Women trafficked from East Asian countries and Bangladesh to the Middle East transit through Pakistan.

The government of Pakistan does not yet fully comply with minimum standards for the elimination of trafficking; however, it is making significant efforts to do so despite severely limited resources and the fact that some of its territory is beyond the control of the government. The government of Pakistan is strongest in prevention and protection. The government should increase training for low-level police officers, prosecutors, and judges throughout the country. Prosecution and conviction of those involved in trafficking should increase over the next year.

The government of Pakistan does not support specific anti-trafficking prevention programs. However, the government supports targeted prevention programs, such as poverty alleviation, eradication of child labor, promotion of girls' education, and women's income generation projects aimed at eradicating the root causes of trafficking. A government child-labor initiative to keep children in school also targets those children and families most susceptible to trafficking. The government started a new program with benchmarks and target dates to eliminate child labor. At the provincial level, the Punjab Ministry of Social Welfare established women's workshops and training centers, offering instruction in legal income-generating activities. The Federal Investigative Agency (FIA) Academy in Islamabad provides trafficking-awareness training.

In October 2002, the government of Pakistan passed a law that criminalizes all aspects of trafficking, from recruitment and transporting to receiving a person. If rape or forced prostitution cases are prosecuted under the Islamic law-oriented Hudood ordinances, victims are often reluctant to testify because the woman's testimony is tantamount to an admission of adultery if prosecutors conclude that her testimony does not meet the burden of proof. The act of adultery in Pakistan is punishable by death.

In Pakistan, law enforcement investigates trafficking cases. The Federal Investigative Agency (FIA) reports that eleven people have been arrested for trafficking under the new statute, and that prosecutions of those individuals are pending. Backlogged courts slow legal proceedings. Pakistan and Iran signed an agreement to conduct joint investigations on trafficking in persons and narcotics. The country worked with Iranian authorities on cases involving the trafficking of camel jockeys. The government is improving its ability to patrol its borders through training and equipment, but large areas of uncontrollable borders allow traffickers to bring women and children into Pakistan. Despite the establishment of a National Accountability Bureau and some noteworthy prosecutions of corruption cases, corruption remains a problem throughout Pakistan.

The government sponsors a variety of shelters and training programs throughout Pakistan that provide medical treatment, limited legal representation, and vocational training. The government provides temporary residence status to foreign trafficking victims, as well as a lawyer on demand. However, without the advocacy of an NGO, victims may be treated as criminals and detained on the basis of their illegal immigration status. Many victims languish in jail for months or years without having their cases heard. On the provincial and local levels, the Punjab Ministry for Social Welfare collaborates with approximately four hundred nongovernmental organizations in providing women's shelters, orphanages, and rehabilitation programs for women and children who have been victims of trafficking. In countries where Pakistani laborers have been trafficked, embassy officials assist those who have been placed in abusive working conditions.

RUSSIA

Russia is a major source country for women who are trafficked to numerous countries for the purpose of sexual exploitation. Russia is also reported to be a transit and destination country for trafficking in persons for sexual and labor exploitation. Reportedly, women from former Soviet countries are transited through Russia to Gulf States, Europe, and North America for the purpose of sexual exploitation. Russia is also increasingly understood as a destination country for labor trafficking, both within the former Soviet Union and from neighboring countries. Internal trafficking is also reported to exist.

Russia is one of the largest traffickers of human beings into the United States. They are noted as a Tier 2 country by the U.S. State Department. The government of Russia does not fully comply with the minimum standards for the elimination of trafficking; however, it is making significant efforts to do so. Efforts made in the reporting period will need to be strengthened in light of the scale of the trafficking problem. Central government officials showed a strong increase in political will to recognize and confront their trafficking problem, and recent efforts to initiate new reforms have been positive.

Russia's legal structure still does not allow for effective prosecution of traffickers, nor for victim assistance, and efforts to prosecute traffickers for related crimes have been largely unsuccessful. The government of Russia must adopt and actively implement both the criminal and protective elements of the proposed legislation, and as a major source country, Russia must focus an effective nationwide prevention campaign.

The government of Russia did not sponsor a comprehensive antitrafficking campaign, but it engaged in a number of awareness events, aimed both at the general public and potential victims. The Deputy Chair of the Duma Legislative Committee led a legislative working group, which conducted a series of national and international conferences to educate various constituents of the antitrafficking community and design a national action plan. The working group participated in more than fifty press events arranged by its press liaison, including placing articles with discussion of trafficking in Russia in major newspapers and magazines. They also conduct discussions on Russian television and radio, and show a dramatic film on the trafficking of a young Russian girl to a cross-section of public professionals and leaders, with educational discussions before and after the film. Regionally, the governments of Irkutsk and Khabarovsk established anti-trafficking in persons commissions, which include information-sharing and research, and some regional governments and police sent their officers to training offered by nongovernmental organizations. In one region, Yekaterinburg, the local government encourages its officers to work with the nongovernmental organizations in prevention programs. The regional response is not directed by the central government, and while the geographic immensity of Russia requires a local government approach, it has not been consistent or widespread.

Russia does not currently have antitrafficking legislation, although it does have legislation against slavery, rape, and falsification of documents. One major obstacle to active investigations and prosecutions has been the lack of laws related to trafficking crimes, and the small number of investigations conducted in the past year mostly failed for lack of evidence. A high-level multi-agency legislative review working group drafted a comprehensive new antitrafficking law criminalizing trafficking in persons and establishing victim assistance and protection. As of April 2003, the criminal trafficking elements were being incorporated into the President's omnibus criminal code revision while the special law proceeded through readings in Parliament.

The government passed a new criminal-procedure code that allows greater protections for victims and witnesses in court proceedings, and that allows prosecution in Russia of Russian citizens who engage in crimes abroad, including trafficking-related crimes. The Prosecutor General's office established a new office to work on international cooperation, mandated to fulfill requests from foreign governments on mutual legal assistance. The Ministry of Internal Affairs cooperated in two ongoing international trafficking investigations with the

United States, and assisted French law enforcement in investigation of a trafficking ring that was dismantled in October 2002.

In 2002, the Governments of Russia and the United States conducted a joint operation against child exploitation and trafficking, resulting in several ongoing investigations in Russia, and some final convictions. Regarding investigations against employment and recruitment agencies, agents of two firms were prosecuted for the preparation of false documents. Police do not respond actively to victims' complaints pursuant to the belief that any criminally proscribed behavior, such as slavery and rape, mostly happens after victims have left their jurisdiction. In the far eastern region, where trafficking from China is a concern, the Ministry of Internal Affairs created a special unit to focus on migration-related crimes and sexual exploitation of migrants, with a particular interest in trafficking. In an effort to decrease the incidence of corruption in the police and judiciary officials, President Putin quadrupled the salary of judges and doubled the salary of police. The government also instituted a Code of Civil Service Behavior in an attempt to prevent corruption.

Nongovernmental organizations active throughout Russia mostly report positive cooperation with local police and the government, but many also report corruption as a major hindrance. The central government does not provide assistance to victims, nor does it support nongovernmental organizations providing assistance, but some regional governments cooperate with local nongovernmental organizations. Central government authorities did not establish a referral mechanism, but some regional governments did, most notably in the high-risk region of Irkutsk. Current federal law provides mechanisms for victim rights and witness protection during court proceedings, including the right to question the defendant and seek compensation from the defendant without filing a separate civil suit. As trafficking in persons is not yet a prosecutable crime, its success cannot yet be measured. Amendments to witness-protection laws will enhance existing protection, and the Ministry of Interior has established a new witness-protection unit.

MEXICO

Mexico is a major source of and transit point for primarily Mexican and Central American migrants traveling to the United States, some of whom are trafficked or at risk of being trafficked for labor or sexual exploitation. Others from Asia, South America, and Eastern Europe transit Mexico to the United States. Those who do not succeed in passing through are often forced into prostitution in Mexico, including a high number of children in the border area near Guatemala. In addition to international trafficking, Mexico has internal trafficking, especially for the sexual exploitation of children.

Mexico is one of the biggest importers of forced laborers in the United States. They are listed as a Tier 2 nation. The government of Mexico does not fully comply with the minimum standards for the elimination of trafficking; however, it is making significant efforts to do so. The government has launched a national campaign against the sexual exploitation of children and has achieved a high level of success in interdicting illicit migration, including trafficking; however, efforts to assist victims and punish traffickers, especially those who sexually exploit minors, are still limited.

Mexico's national campaign against sexual exploitation of children, which urges people to report the crime, has begun to show positive results. Continued and increased efforts to raise awareness under this initiative will help identify and assist a greater number of victims.

Mexico's record on law enforcement against trafficking is uneven. There have been great successes, including the significant reduction of illicit migration and trafficking in persons between Baja California and the United States, thanks to excellent cooperation between Mexican and U.S. officials. However, in other areas, such as Ciudad Juarez, which reports a high incidence of child prostitution and child pornography, investigation has been weak. Enforcement may improve in Ciudad Juarez, as the federal social welfare agency recently contributed to a study of the problem, and nongovernmental organizations have begun sensitivity training for police. In Tapachula, near the Guatemalan border, brothel owners have trafficked hundreds of Central American minors into prostitution with almost complete impunity. Mexico continues to improve its efforts to monitor its borders well in many places. In 2001, border officials turned back 15,000 undocumented aliens and hundreds of migrant smugglers, and in 2002, federal police arrested the head of an international alien-smuggling network. Some of these were traffickers and victims, but no data is available on the scope of the crime for two main reasons: 1) Mexico is primarily a transit country, so the extent of trafficking may not be evident until the victim reaches the destination; and 2) Mexican officials do not attempt to distinguish between victims or traffickers; they simply deport them all. Corruption and poor enforcement against exploiters of children weaken Mexico's prosecution efforts.

The Mexican government's social welfare agency

assists trafficking victims repatriated from the United States by providing them with shelters and healthcare, and by returning victims to their families. The availability and quality of these programs varies widely by region. The federal government occasionally funds nongovernmental organizations to assist victims, but overall the level of government services should be expanded to meet the current need. Foreign victims of trafficking who are found living in Mexico illegally are generally deported instead of being given public assistance and the chance to help prosecutors develop a case against their traffickers.

THE PEOPLE'S REPUBLIC OF CHINA

The People's Republic of China (PRC) is a source, transit, and destination country for trafficking for labor and sexual exploitation. There is also internal trafficking of young women and girls to be sold as brides. Victims trafficked into the PRC originate from Thailand, Burma, Mongolia, Laos, North Korea, Vietnam, and Russia; they are most often young women and girls trafficked for prostitution or sold as brides. Political prisoners in the PRC, including Tibetans, are occasionally forced to work in prison and detention facilities. Chinese are trafficked to Taiwan, Singapore, Australia, Japan, Malaysia, the Hong Kong or Macau Special Administrative Regions, South Korea, North America, and Europe. Many Chinese migrants who are smuggled to North America become trapped in forced labor to repay traffickers.

The government of the PRC does not fully comply with the minimum standards for the elimination of trafficking; however, it is making significant efforts to do so. Senior officials have expressed their determination to combat trafficking, and policies are in place to do so. Although the implementation of those policies is uneven, the PRC's continued high-level engagement of fighting trafficking is vital to address the worldwide problem. The PRC can sharpen its effectiveness by widening its international cooperation on law enforcement. The government should continue to fight corruption along its lengthy borders.

The PRC has continued public-awareness campaigns against trafficking in women and children, including warning messages about abuses of domestic brides. The Ministry of Public Security (MPS) announced its four-year "Elimination of Trafficking: Zero-Tolerance Plan" with UNICEF targeting rural farmers via promoting awareness and educational activities. MPS drafted an antitrafficking action plan that established a national committee to oversee its development. Other campaigns were aimed at keeping children in school ("Spring Bud Plan") and women's empowerment ("Rural Women Know All") through vocational training and rights awareness. The ILO-IPEC Mekong Sub-Regional Project continues to prevent trafficking through cooperation between government officials and local communities.

Trafficking in women is specifically outlawed in the PRC. The government recognizes trafficking as a priority law enforcement issue and has an antitrafficking unit within the MPS. No government figures were released on prosecutions for the past year, although press releases note that there were 469 arrests of suspected human traffickers in the Fujian province alone. Intergovernment cooperation and exchanges between law enforcement officials have taken place with Vietnam and Thailand.

PRC assistance is primarily focused on Chinese trafficking victims. Women are reintegrated into their communities through resettlement centers that offer legal, medical, and psychological help. The PRC collaborated with UNICEF on three pilot transit centers that offer victims temporary lodging, counseling, and vocational training, as well as train hundreds of MPS officers on victims' needs.

ISRAEL

Israel, a Tier 2 nation state, is a destination country for trafficked persons. Women from Moldova, Russia, Ukraine, and other countries in the former Soviet Union are trafficked to Israel for the purpose of commercial sexual exploitation. Persons in search of work are trafficked into situations of forced labor, in which they endure physical abuse or other extreme working conditions. Many low-skilled foreign workers in Israel have their passports withheld, their contracts altered, and suffer nonpayment of salaries of varying degree and duration. Construction firms and other businesses have brought male laborers from China and Bulgaria into Israel to work under conditions equivalent to debt bondage or involuntary servitude.

The government of Israel does not fully comply with the minimum standards for the elimination of trafficking; however, it is making significant efforts to do so. Although the government has pursued numerous cases of trafficking for the purpose of sexual exploitation, it must continue taking steps to combat trafficking for forced labor and sexual exploitation. Labor trafficking is a relatively new phenomenon in Israel, and the government should increase its efforts to prosecute those involved in perpetrating labor trafficking in upcoming years. The government should ensure that employers comply with labor regulations, protect the rights of migrant workers, and curb fraud associated with issuance of work permits.

The government of Israel, in conjunction with nongovernmental organizations, has undertaken public-awareness campaigns that include the development and distribution in Israel of fliers and other information in Russian on trafficking for commercial sexual exploitation. It is also using its consulates and embassies in source countries to provide information to potential victims of sex trafficking.

Israeli law criminalizes trafficking in persons for purposes of sexual and labor exploitation. Other charges, such as rape, false imprisonment, retaining a passport, forced labor, prostitution by means of coercion or fraud, and kidnapping for the purpose of prostitution, may also be brought. The maximum penalty for aggravated trafficking or trafficking of a minor is twenty years in prison, and the penalties proscribed by law are commensurate with those for rape and assault; however, the majority of cases are resolved through plea bargains that result, on the average, in sentences of about two years. Law enforcement actively investigates allegations of trafficking for sexual exploitation, and last year opened sixty-seven investigations of one hundred and thirty-eight people and arrested ninety-two suspects. The government prosecuted some thirty cases resulting in twenty-eight plea bargains, many of which carried sentences ranging from six months to nine years, as well as fines. The government also is investigating individual policemen for taking bribes or tipping off brothels about raids, but these instances of corruption are not widespread. A small cadre of dedicated officials works to combat trafficking, but low staffing and funding hamper the officials' efforts. The Ministry of Justice held antitrafficking seminars for prosecutors and police. To combat labor trafficking, the Immigration Authority was established in September 2002 to coordinate government activity related to foreign nationals, including the investigation of offenses against migrant workers. Labor laws determining minimum wage, guaranteed pay, and annual leave apply to all workers in Israel, but enforcement measures are mainly directed toward migrant workers, not their employers, who sometimes openly breach the law. The Immigration Authority has an investigation unit that has uncovered several networks of criminals involved in document forgery and fraud. Prosecutors recently filed an indictment against four suspects allegedly involved in abusing workers from Bulgaria. Israel exercises strict control and supervision of its borders.

Victims of trafficking for commercial sexual exploitation who are willing to testify against their traffickers are housed in police-funded hostels, and are provided full board, pocket money, and access to medical care. Victims who are unwilling to testify are deported. Victims are not prosecuted or fined for offenses material to their trafficking, such as illegal entry or forged documentation. Police actively encourage victims to file complaints against their traffickers. The government partially funds a hotline. Regulations stipulate that migrant workers who report a criminal offense are not detained, are allowed access to an interpreter, and may stay in Israel as witnesses during a criminal trial; some nongovernmental organizations allege that these regulations are sometimes violated.

REPUBLIC OF SOUTH KOREA

South Korea is a source, transit, and destination country for women who are trafficked for sexual exploitation. Victims come mainly from Southeast Asia (particularly the Philippines and Thailand), China, Russia, Uzbekistan, and Kazakhstan. Women often enter South Korea on "entertainer" visas and are forced to work as prostitutes in bars and private clubs. South Korean women are also trafficked abroad to Japan and the United States.

The government of South Korea fully complies with the minimum standards for the elimination of trafficking. The government recognizes that trafficking is a national problem and undertakes comprehensive efforts to prevent it, protect victims, and prosecute traffickers. The government's decision to apply stricter standards in the issuance of "entertainer" visas is a positive move and will require further monitoring. The government has also taken important steps to reduce police corruption associated with trafficking.

Many government agencies undertake education and prevention campaigns. The Korean National Police Agency prints materials in various languages, explaining the dangers of trafficking and detailing the assistance and services offered to victims by the government. Thousands of police officers visit schools to discuss trafficking issues with children. The highest-ranking female police officer in South Korea has reached out to foreign embassies and potential trafficking victims. South Korean embassies in countries where women have been trafficked distribute leaflets warning visa applicants of sex trafficking.

South Korea has no antitrafficking law, but it uses a variety of criminal statutes to prosecute traffickers. In 2002, the government reported that it detained and investigated four hundred and fifty suspected traffickers, indicted ninety, and convicted sixty-eight perpetrators. Penalties varied based on the criminal statute applied, but three years was the average sentence. South Korea cooperates internationally on law enforcement, working with Interpol and the governments of other nations to identify and arrest traffickers. Senior police officials have addressed incidents of corruption in their lower ranks, and two Korean consular officials were recently indicted for accepting bribes to issue visas.

Government protection efforts in South Korea are comprehensive, and officials are aware of the need to protect victims of trafficking. The Ministry of Gender Equality provides assistance for temporary and long-term shelters, which offer trafficking victims free lodging and food, medical assistance, counseling, and legal services. The government also provides funding to domestic nongovernmental organizations, which offer victims shelter. The rights of foreign victims are generally respected, and they are not charged with illegal employment or residency. Victims are provided free legal services so they can seek compensation for unpaid wages. When trafficking victims report a crime or act as a witness in court, their identities and personal information are kept confidential for their protection.

FORMER YUGOSLAV REPUBLIC OF MACEDONIA

Macedonia is a country of transit and destination for women and children trafficked for prostitution from the former Soviet Union and Eastern Europe, notably

Ukraine, Moldova, Romania, and Bulgaria. Some victims remain in Macedonia, while others are trafficked to Albania, Kosovo, or Italy.

The government of Macedonia fully complies with the minimum standards for the elimination of trafficking. The government showed increasingly effective law enforcement activities in ethnic Albanian areas that were not under government control during the 2001 conflict, and in areas where trafficking activity is prevalent. As a post-conflict country with limited resources, it focused significant efforts on combating trafficking. The low conviction rate relative to arrests has emerged as an area of concern, and numerous press and public reports were published questioning the integrity of members of the judiciary department. In the next year efforts should continue to strengthen the judiciary department's capacity to enforce the rule of law. Macedonia is listed as a Tier I state by the U.S. State Department.

The government of Macedonia cosponsored with the International Organization for Migration and local nongovernmental organizations several preventive events, including a public-awareness campaign, and a focused campaign in the country's third largest city. The interministerial National Anti-Trafficking Committee, headed by the Ministry of Interior State Secretary, oversees implementation of the National Action Plan. The government instituted a new policy on the issuance of work permits, whereby a centralized policy review board approves all work permit requests. Requests for permits for dancers and waitresses are given strict review, and most are denied. The government continues to participate actively in Stability Pact regional ministerial meetings and capacity-building programs.

Criminal articles that forbid organized and forced prostitution are used to prohibit and punish trafficking in persons. During the reporting period, courts handed down eleven convictions, ranging from six months to seven years. Police increased their ability to investigate and arrest traffickers in areas of previously limited government control, and the government filed more than seventy trafficking-related charges against more than one hundred perpetrators. The government arrested and prosecuted notorious trafficking kingpin Dilaver Bojku and of his two associates. For activities conducted before enactment of the current antitrafficking legislation, the applicable criminal article held a maximum penalty of only one year; the court handed Bojku a six-month sentence in Ohrid Jail. He was transferred to a prison halfway house, during which time the Ministry of Interior secured additional trafficking charges against him and extended his detention, pending trial. The government routinely cooperates with neighboring countries through its Southeastern Cooperative Initiative (SECI) liaison and through its bilateral cooperation agreements with UN authorities in Kosovo, Serbia, Montenegro, and Bulgaria. Government efforts to crack down on corruption continued, and several internal investigations are ongoing. In 2003, charges were brought against a local police official for trafficking and other crimes, and the case is proceeding through the court system.

Macedonian police routinely place victims found

during antitrafficking raids in the government's transit shelter for trafficking victims. Once the victims are in the transitional shelter, a local nongovernmental organization conducts interviews, and they are offered repatriation, counseling, and medical and other support services through the International Organization for Migration. During the reporting period, 292 foreign female victims were processed through the shelter, twenty-three of whom were under eighteen. Victims of trafficking in Macedonia do not receive temporary residency status. While the government was working to enact a witness-protection law and program, the police and the International Organization for Migration provided ad hoc witness protection for some witnesses who were willing to testify. Police and prosecutors also receive training on trafficking.

THE NETHERLANDS

The Netherlands is currently a Tier I state. It is both a significant destination and transit country for trafficking, most notably for the purposes of sexual exploitation, although there is also labor trafficking there. Most victims originate from Central and Eastern Europe, primarily Bulgaria, the Czech Republic, the Russian Federation, Ukraine, and Moldova, and also from African countries, primarily Nigeria. According to some experts, the number of reported trafficking victims brought to the Netherlands, almost all foreign, has more than quadrupled over the past decade, rising from 70 to 341.

The government of the Netherlands fully complies with the minimum standards for the elimination of trafficking. The government has numerous and sophisticated prevention, prosecution, and protection programs. However, the lack of a specific law against and punishment for forced labor trafficking, lack of punishment of equal severity for sex trafficking compared to other grave sex crimes, and limited outreach by the government to the large number of foreign victims of sex trafficking warrant concern.

The government of the Netherlands does not conduct prevention campaigns targeting the demand for illegal sex services within the public at large, but it subsidizes numerous nongovernmental organization information campaigns in Dutch schools and youth clubs. Dutch nongovernmental organizations complain of insufficient efforts to target source countries, but the government engages in bilateral assistance to many countries and sponsors preventative education programs. Most impressively, the government funds a National Rapporteur on Trafficking in Human Beings, who investigates trafficking and publishes in-depth reports on the findings.

Trafficking for the purpose of sexual exploitation is specifically prohibited and subject to punishment in the Netherlands. But while the standard punishment for rape is twelve years in prison, the punishment for trafficking for sexual exploitation is six years in prison with more severe penalties for aggravating circumstances, such as the trafficking of a minor. The average sentence for trafficking for sexual exploitation alone is even lower: eighteen months. A law that prohibits and punishs other forms of trafficking, such as for forced labor, and protects victims of forced labor, was introduced but has not been adopted as of

April 2003. There is a national public prosecutor for sex trafficking and an antitrafficking coordinator in each district court. Sex trafficking is reportedly a high priority for police in many regions of the country. Approximately 217 cases were prosecuted last year, showing an increase from the previous year. While there were no reported convictions, the number of cases resulting in sentences was quite high in previous years. According to the Dutch Rapporteur, the majority of foreign victims do not usually avail themselves of the government's B-9 immigration law, which allows the victim to remain in the country for three months while pursuing prosecution. This is probably due to a lack of knowledge, unequal access to legal counsel, fear of retribution, and restrictions on employment during this period.

The government of the Netherlands subsidizes various Dutch and foreign nongovernmental organizations that work with victims that have been trafficked for sexual exploitation, and the Dutch government cooperates with the governments of source countries. Most shelters are designed for Dutch victims of domestic violence, but they seek to address the needs of all victims. The Health Ministry assisted in publishing a manual that instructs relief workers about the rights of foreign victims. Special shelters have been set up for underage foreign victims, but victim's rights organizations have called for additional measures.

COLOMBIA

Colombia is a major source of women and girls who are trafficked into prostitution. Victims are primarily sent to Europe, especially Spain and the Netherlands, as well as Japan. There also is internal trafficking in Colombia for prostitution and forced conscription in terrorist and guerrilla groups, often with children as victims. Colombia is listed as a Tier I country by the U.S. State Department.

The government of Colombia fully complies with the minimum standards for the elimination of trafficking. The widespread internal armed conflict, the existence of well-organized drug-trafficking groups, and economic pressures combine to make Colombia one of the major source countries for trafficking victims in Latin America. However, despite these factors, the government continues to make serious and sustained efforts toward the elimination of trafficking in persons, both at home and abroad.

A Colombian interagency committee coordinates a variety of antitrafficking prevention measures, including the creation of a hotline, public-awareness campaigns, and improved coordination with Interpol. Police and immigration officials, with the help of nongovernmental organizations, closely monitor airports and have prevented dozens of Colombians from being trafficked by identifying would-be victims and educating them on the dangers that lay ahead.

In 2002, improved antitrafficking legislation in Colombia broadened the definition of trafficking and toughened the penalties—almost doubling prison sentences and raising the maximum fine by a factor of ten. Colombia is one of the leading countries engaged in international law enforcement cooperation against trafficking. Police have conducted numerous international operations in coordination with other governments, particularly Spain, the Netherlands, and Japan, which have led to the rescue of hundreds of trafficking victims and more than one hundred arrests. For example, in November 2002, information provided by Colombian law enforcement authorities through Colombia's diplomatic mission in Tokyo led Japanese officials to arrest a major organized-crime leader who had trafficked at least four hundred Colombian women into Japan. Several Colombian collaborators in the trafficking ring were deported to Colombia, where they are under indictment and in custody. Domestically, police are proactive, attempting to break up trafficking rings before women are victimized. In the last eighteen months, government authorities have arrested forty-four persons on trafficking charges, indicted thirty, and convicted sixteen. The government encourages victims to testify against traffickers, but the witness-protection program is underfunded, and successful intimidation by traffickers has limited the number of successful prosecutions.

The Ministry of Foreign Affairs assists Colombian victims abroad by providing basic services and facilitating repatriation. The government cooperates with a network of nongovernmental organizations and the International Organization for Migration to provide support and assistance to victims once they return to Colombia. The government works with the International Organization for Migration to train diplomats and consular officials on how to assist victims. The International Organization for Migration also works closely with other governmental officials, training more than five hundred officials last year on the implementation of the new trafficking law.

CZECH REPUBLIC

The Czech Republic is a source, transit, and destination country for women who are trafficked from the former Soviet Union (in particular, Russia, Belarus, Ukraine, and Moldova), Eastern Europe, the Balkans, and Asia into the Czech Republic and onward to Western Europe and the United States for prostitution. Small numbers of Czech men are trafficked to the United States for forced labor. There is some evidence of internal trafficking of Czech women and children from areas of low employment near border regions with Germany and Austria. Additionally, foreign minors are believed to be exploited in the commercial sex trade either in the Czech Republic or other European countries.

The government of the Czech Republic fully complies with the minimum standards for the elimination of trafficking. The government has focused its resources on all three areas, especially prioritizing regional law enforcement cooperation. However, information on court convictions was uneven, and a lack of resources has hampered some overall efforts.

The Crime Prevention Division of the Interior Ministry implemented a national media campaign on the dangers of trafficking, as well as an informational program in Czech schools, targeting thirteen- and fourteen-year-olds. The government created a National Plan for Combating Commercial Sexual Abuse, including trafficking in women and children for sexual purposes, for which the Interior Ministry has the leading role.

The government amended the criminal code to include a broader definition of trafficking victims, and to raise the penalty from five to twelve years for traffickers who cause grave bodily harm to their victims. In 2002, the Czech Republic investigated nineteen cases under the trafficking in persons statute, yielding fourteen indictments. While none of the cases have been concluded, eight individuals were held in pretrial detention pending final resolution. Police recorded 139 trafficking-related arrests during 2002. The Anti-Organized Crime Police has a special unit specifically trained in human trafficking, and the Interior Ministry cooperates closely with nongovernmental organizations to train police and investigators who handle trafficking cases. The government cooperates with regional governments to investigate and prosecute trafficking cases. The Foreigner and Border Police work closely with their counterparts in Germany and Austria, and in June 2002, Czech authorities conducted a series of raids on suspected traffickers with counterparts in Germany, Austria, Bulgaria, and Romania. Border monitoring is relatively weaker regarding the Polish and Slovak borders, but the government is using European Union assistance to improve its border control.

The government refers trafficking victims to nongovernmental organizations, which provide shelter and medical treatment; the government also provides partial funding for these services. The Interior Ministry funds a nongovernmental organization that assists foreign victims with repatriation and Czech victims with reintegration services. Victims who are willing to testify against a trafficker may be offered temporary residence, a work permit, access to social assistance, and, in extreme cases, police protection. The government continues to detain some possible victims, followed by removal either immediately or after a thirty-day stay of deportation.

COMBATING TRAFFICKING

All of the previous examples illuminate how truly difficult it is to battle this grotesque problem, but U.S. policy-makers and other leading economic countries are attempting to take action.

"In the last three years, the U.S. has made historic progress in creating new tools to combat trafficking in women and children," Donna M. Hughes, Ph.D. Professor and Carlson Endowed Chair in Women's Studies at the University of Rhode Island reported to the Subcommittee of East Asian and Pacific Affairs Senate Foreign Relations Committee on April 9, 2003. "In 2000, Congress passed the Trafficking Victims Protection Act, which created new laws with which to fight the traffickers and provided new services for victims. It authorized the creation of The Office to Monitor and Combat Trafficking in Persons. That office is now fully functional and under...capable leadership."

She also reported that in December 2002, the Department of Justice's Office of Juvenile Justice and Delinquency Prevention held the first national conference on child prostitution. According to Hughes, a number of speakers addressed trafficking of girls and boys to the U.S. for prostitution.

In February 2003, President Bush signed a

National Security Presidential Directive on trafficking in persons. Activists who have been working against the sexual abuse and exploitation of women and children for years are pleased that it is now U.S. policy that prostitution and related activities are considered "inherently harmful and dehumanizing" and are recognized as "contribut[ing] to the phenomenon of trafficking in persons and sex tourism. This policy directive is especially crucial in fighting trafficking in women and children because over the past decade there have been attempts to de-link trafficking from prostitution, and even to legitimize prostitution as a form of work for women.

"The U.S. Agency for International Development was quick to respond by announcing a new 'Anti-Trafficking Strategy,'" which states that 'organizations advocating prostitution as an employment choice or which advocate or support the legalization of prostitution are not appropriate partners for USAID anti-trafficking grants or contracts.' Kent Hill and his staff in USAID's Bureau for Europe and Eurasia have been open to finding ways to combat the trafficking and prostitution of women and children," Hughes continued. "The challenge now is to implement these landmark policies in order to free women and children from enslavement."

Assessment of National Efforts to Combat Trafficking
Rankings by U.S. State Department 2002

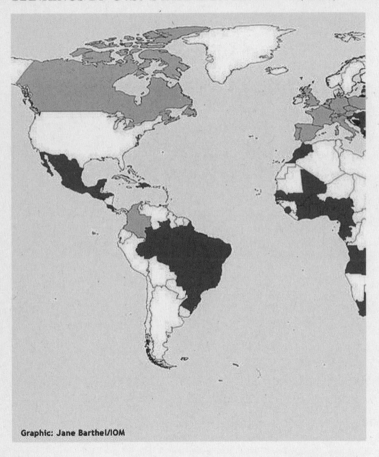

Graphic: Jane Barthel/IOM

"Victims of Trafficking and Violence Protection Act of 2000: Trafficking in Persons Report," June 2002, United States, State Department, June 2002. Map illustrates countries where victims of human trafficking are recruited. The map highlights Tier One (countries who fulfill their minimum requirements), Tier Two (those countries who have deficiencies, but who report progress); and Tier Three who have made unsatisfactory progress toward meeting the minimum standards.
Courtesy U.S. State Department, 2002.

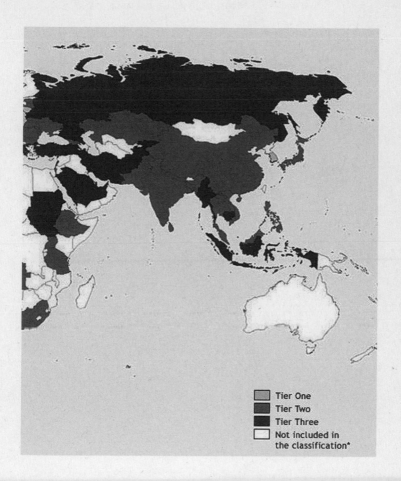

Tier One
Tier Two
Tier Three
Not included in
the classification*

Conclusion

"There has to be a real concerted effort. What...others need to do in the media, in law enforcement, is to make it clear that this is a crime. That we will punish to the hilt of the law. And we're not going to rest until we do everything possible to eliminate it from our shores, at least," U.S. Senator Hillary Rodham Clinton told Jamie Rubin of PBS Wide Angle, "Dying to Leave" (9/25/03).

One of the major problems law enforcement and human-rights advocates face in their efforts to combat human trafficking is the public's perception of trafficking itself. Some continue to view prostitution as a victimless crime involving willing participants, never understanding that consent is irrelevant when it comes to human trafficking. Others only see the immigration or worker-exploitation angles in trafficking. Even the Immigration and Naturalization Service (INS) has been known to jump to the conclusion that victims of human trafficking are merely alien-smuggling cases. Consequently, efforts often are made to deport these women rather than investigate the true nature of their presence in the United States.

From a prosecutorial point of view, the challenges are far greater, as it is extremely difficult to infiltrate many of the small, ethnic criminal enterprises that engage in these activities. Traffickers usually instill so much fear of deportation and violence in their victims that the victims are often reluctant to cooperate with police or testify in a trial. And in comparison with sentences given to convicted drug traffickers, those who are convicted in trafficking humans receive, on the whole, much lighter sentences. For example, according to the 1999 CIA report on trafficking in women, several recent human trafficking cases in the United States demonstrated brutally violent treatment of women and children and led to convictions, but the defendants received limited jail time. In Los Angeles, traffickers kidnapped a Chinese woman, raped her, and then forced her into prostitution. She was under constant guard and received cigarette burns as punishment. The lead defendant in this case received just four years' prison time, and the other defendants were sentenced to two to three years.

In a 1996 trafficking case in Maryland, a Russian-American business owner ran ads luring young Russian and Ukranian women for jobs as au pairs and waitresses. When they arrived, he forced them to live in a massage parlor he owned and provide sexual services for clients. In his plea bargain arrangement, he agreed not to operate a business again in that county, and charges against him were dropped. The women, who had never been paid but were charged for their housing, were either deported or left the United States on their own.

Another challenge in investigating and prosecuting human trafficking cases is that there are few resources in place for housing and protecting victims once they are discovered. In fact, many victims are simply placed in INS detention facilities and then deported before investigators have a chance to build a case. On a global scale, the problems are magnified significantly. Poverty, economic depression and lack of education in the dangers and the risks of human trafficking are just a few of the factors that contribute to the growing number of enslaved people around the world. The increasing rates of sexually transmitted diseases such as HIV in many of the countries where human trafficking is most prevalent is just one of the complex issues nations and advocacy groups must face in the twenty-first century. Repeatedly, trafficked women are viewed in many nations as perpetrators of the transmission of HIV and other diseases rather as than the victims themselves.

TRAFFICKING AND AIDS

"Women and children who are trafficked are at high risk for infection with HIV, which is a death sentence for the victims. Brothels and other sites where women and children are used in prostitution are markets for the distribution of the AIDS virus. Awareness of this has led many aid agencies to target brothels for campaigns to increase the use of condoms. This approach requires aid workers to interact and negotiate with pimps and traffickers - some of the worst criminals and human rights violators in the world - in order to gain access to the women and children," Donna M. Hughes, Ph.D. Professor and Carlson Endowed Chair in Women's Studies at the University of Rhode Island reported to the Subcommittee of East Asian and Pacific Affairs Senate Foreign Relations Committee on April 9, 2003.

According to Hughes, in places such as Thailand, some aid programs claimed that a 100% condom use policy resulted in lowering the incidence of AIDS. However, it came at the cost of overlooking or excusing sex slave trading in women and children. This approach sacrifices the safety and freedom of women and children for the eventual good of public health. "Of course, we need programs to prevent the spread of HIV, but we must place the freedom and safety of women and children over the distribution of condoms.

It is unacceptable to provide medical services and condoms to enslaved people and ignore the slavery," Hughes said.

"We should be requiring aid workers to report the abuse, exploitation, and enslavement of women and children to the appropriate authorities. Admittedly, police and officials are sometimes complicit in trafficking and even profit from sexual slavery. Nonetheless, aid workers should be obligated to report, not ignore, slavery. They should also be obligated to catalyze a rescue either through notification of the appropriate authorities or a nongovernmental organization or faith based group that specializes in rescuing women and children enslaved in prostitution.

"We can better reduce the spread of HIV by rescuing trafficking victims and ending the sexual slave trade that creates a demand for more victims. In every case, U.S. policies should encourage the arrest and prosecution of traffickers and pimps and the permanent closure of the brothels.

"There are billions of dollars being spent on

HIV/AIDS prevention and treatment, and a significant portion of it is directed for prevention in 'high risk' groups, such as women and children in prostitution. There should be appropriate restrictions or requirements for how aid organizations and their personnel respond when they suspect that anyone they come in contact with is abused, exploited, or enslaved."

LINKING TRAFFICKING TO PROSTITUTION

Hughes went on to say in her testimony that she thought it imperative "to re-link trafficking to prostitution. For decades, international bodies and instruments recognized the connection between prostitution and trafficking to meet the demand for women and children created by prostitution. Over the past decade, those who want to normalize and legalize prostitution have acted to de-link prostitution and trafficking, as if one did not depend on the other."

Hughes pointed out that the Trafficking Victims Protection Act criminalizes severe forms of trafficking, and that the Trafficking in Persons Report, which is issued annually by the State Department, evaluates and ranks countries on their efforts to combat severe forms of trafficking. She urged Congress "to create a way to analyze the harm of prostitution and the role tolerance and legalization of prostitution plays in the trafficking of women and children."

Hughes pointed out that "worldwide there is an ongoing effort to normalize prostitution. United Nations organizations that receive significant financial support from the United States publicly advocate for this shift in the status of prostitution. For example, in 1998 the International Labor Organization (ILO) released a report called The Sex Sector-The Economic and Social Bases of Prostitution in Southeast Asia. Based on research and analysis of prostitution industries in Malaysia, Indonesia, Thailand and the Philippines, the ILO called for prostitution and sex industries to be officially recognized as a legitimate economic sector because they are already 'integrated into the economic, social and political life' of countries and 'contribute in no small measure to employment, national income and economic growth.'"

She also revealed that in the report, the ILO

pointed out prostitution and sex tourism as a source of foreign income:

> "[The sex sector] is a significant source of foreign exchange earnings, with links between the growth of prostitution as a highly structured transnational business and the expansion of the tourist industry in these countries, as well as labour exports from these countries."

Hughes's testimony also included a jab at the World Health Organization, which she cited as having "a long history of hiring some of the leading advocates for the legalization of prostitution to advise them on policy. In 2001, the World Health Organization recommended the decriminalization of prostitution, claiming that the normalization of prostitution would assist in the fight against the spread of HIV."

U.S. MILITARY AND THE TRAFFICKING OF WOMEN

The U.S. military also plays an unwitting role in the trafficking of women for sex. For example, there are documented cases of women in South Korea from the Philippines, the Russian Federation, Bolivia, Peru, Mongolia, China, Bangladesh, Kyrgyzstan, and Uzbekistan that were being trafficked into bars and clubs around the U.S. bases. According to Hughes, in 2002, "a TV reporter filmed U.S. military police patrolling bars and brothels that held trafficked women. And an investigative reporter for *Navy Times* documented that military police have friendly relations with pimps and bar owners where there are trafficked women."

Of course, engaging in prostitution is a violation of the U.S. Military Code of Conduct. However, it is widely acknowledged by many in the U.S. armed services that this rule is widely ignored. According to Hughes, "The U.S. military has a shameful history in Southeast Asia of fueling the growth of sex industries around military bases or at sites of R&R (rest and relaxation). When the U.S. leaves the area, such as the Philippines, the pimps and traffickers do not shut down their criminal activity, but turn to sex tourism for their revenue. Not only does the demand for prostitution result in the trafficking of women for use in these bars and clubs, the negative local reaction to the abuse and exploitation of women by U.S. military personnel provides fodder for anti-American sentiment and interests."

Hughes pointed out that the government and the Pentagon need to crack down on these kinds of problem areas, if we are to win the war against this kind of human trafficking.

DOMESTIC/INTERNAL TRAFFICKING
WITHIN THE UNITED STATES

This is sometimes referred to as either '"domestic trafficking" or "internal trafficking." Many are now aware of the phenomena of transnational trafficking of women from country to country. But this same inexplicable horror replicates itself within the borders of countries as well, including the United States. According to Hughes, "The Trafficking Victims Protection Acts ensures that trafficked women and children are treated as victims, not as criminals, and provides services they need to recover from their ordeal. The same recognition and services are needed for women and children whose experiences meet all the criteria of a trafficking victim, except that they are U.S. citizens. We will not have succeeded in eradicating the trafficking of women and children until we attend to the victims within our own borders."

Perhaps there is no greater obstacle in combating human trafficking than the cultural tolerance that exists in economically undeveloped nations. In many countries where trafficking flourishes, the belief that all people are created equal does not exist, and those who are viewed as less-then-equal in these societies may be treated in a subhuman manner, because those societies believe it is their karmic fate. In short, there are many in this world who do not consider the selling of human beings to be inherently wrong. This fact alone illustrates the difficulty the world will face in trying to stamp out the new slave trade—a crisis of humanity that rings of the Dark Ages, not the twenty-first century.

"It's the dark underbelly of globalization," U.S. Senator Hillary Rodham Clinton told Jamie Rubin of

PBS Wide Angle. "Now that we can move goods and people with such ease all over the world, it is very hard to know what it is that we are transporting, where it's supposed to end up. This is true for human beings, it's true for drugs, it's true for weapons, it's true for terrorism, it is something we have to come to grips with. I think we should be looking at trafficking, not only as an evil, in and of itself, that the world has to combat, but as part of some of the problems that we face because of globalization."

APPENDIX I

MATRIX OF SOME OF THE MAJOR TRAFFICKING CASES IN THE UNITED STATES OVER THE LAST EIGHT YEARS, CASE SUMMARIES

In the last three years, the Department of Justice has prosecuted numerous modern-dayslavery and trafficking cases. The Department's Involuntary Servitude Coordinator alone has prosecuted slavery cases involving over 150 victims. These trafficking cases involved varying degrees of deception, confinement, force, and grievous human rights abuses. These cases were not specific to one region, having occurred around the country. These cases do not offer an exhaustive list of prosecutions, as they do not list state law enforcement efforts. They do provide, however, a glimpse into the civil rights violations and US government efforts to combat them.

U.S. v. CADENA 1998

Background: From about February 1996 to about March 1998, some 25 to 40 Mexican women and girls, some as young as 14 years old, were trafficked from the Veracruz state in Mexico to Florida and the Carolinas in the United States. The victims had been promised jobs in waitressing, housekeeping, landscaping, childcare and elder care. Upon their arrival, the women and girls were told they must work as prostitutes in brothels serving migrant workers or risk harm to themselves and/or their families.

Confinement: Besides enduring threats, women who attempted to escape were subjugated to beatings. Guards used force to keep them in the brothels in order that they pay off their smuggling debt that ranged from $2,000 to $3,000. One woman was locked in a closet for 15 days as punishment for trying to escape. Additional human rights abuses included: forced prostitution, assault, rape, and forced abortions.

Outcome: In March 1998, 16 men were indicted in Florida for enslaving the Mexican women and girls in brothels. The men were charged with importing aliens for immoral purposes, transporting women and minors for prostitution, involuntary servitude, visa fraud, conspiracy, and violation of civil rights. The defendants' sentences ranged from 2 to 6 years, with one ringleader receiving 15 years. The judge ordered that the trafficking organization pay $1 million dollars in restitution. Several of the other key ringleaders had previously fled to Mexico. The United States is working with the Mexican government to secure their capture. The victims, who are currently living in Florida at either a shelter or on their own, did receive some money from the traffickers seized assets in the US.

U.S. v. MISHULOVICH 1999

Background: From around October 1996 to August 1997, a Russian-American named Alexander

Mishulovich was involved in large scale visa fraud, recruiting Latvian women in Riga to come to Chicago, Illinois to dance in bikinis in respectable, sophisticated nightclubs. The women were told that they would earn significant sums of money ($60,000 a year) and there would be no nudity. Mishulovich instructed the women to falsely represent their intentions when presenting themselves to the American Embassy. Upon arrival however, the women were forced to dance topless and nude. He took the women's passports and visas, which he offered to sell back to them for up to $60,000. Later on, he ultimately sold the passports back to some of the women for $4,000 in cash.

Confinement: The women were not permitted to return to Latvia without paying off their smuggling debt. The women were also locked in apartments or hotel rooms, routinely beaten, and maltreated to secure their continued cooperation. Mishulovich and his co-conspirators took through force and threats the money the young women earned from 139 The information on the major trafficking cases listed below comes from a variety of sources, most notably from the Department of Justice, Civil Rights Division, Criminal Section and INS headquarters. It is not an exhaustive list of the trafficking and slavery cases in the United States. dancing. Mishulovich threatened to kill the young women and their family members through his extensive organized crime connections if the women failed to accede to his demands.

Outcome: On September 10, 1998 Mishulovich, another Russian, and two Latvians were arrested for a variety of offenses including peonage, conspiracy to commit offense or fraud, and obstructing law enforcement. The arrests also resulted in the recovery of II weapons, ammunition, documents, and photographs identifying additional victims. The case is scheduled to go to trial this December. Two to three of the victims returned home voluntarily while others are living in the US on their own while awaiting the trial.

U.S. v. KWON 1998

Background: From on or about June 1995 until on or about January 1998, defendants recruited and transported Chinese-Korean women from China to the Commonwealth of the Northern Mariana Islands for the purpose of exploiting and abusing them for profit. They were promised legitimate waitressing jobs but then forced to work at a karaoke club and submit to customer's sexual demands. Some of the women also complained of physical and sexual abuse by their bosses.

Confinement: The women were held at a barracks apartment. The defendants took their passports, visas, and airline tickets. The women were only allowed to leave the barracks apartment with permission and an escort. The women were threatened with violence, including death, if they left or attempted to leave without paying their debt.

Outcome: Three defendants were indicted on November 1998 for conspiracy against rights, involuntary servitude, extortion, transportation for illegal sexual activity, and the use of a firearm in the commission of a crime of violence. They pled guilty to conspiracy to violate the 13th Amendment and laws governing involuntary servitude, extortion, and transportation for illegal sexual purposes. Their sentences will likely range from 2 to 8 years. The victims are currently living on their own in apartments in Guam working at jobs the Department of Justice helped them acquire.

U.S. v. MILAN LEJHANEC AND LADISLAV RUC 1998

Background: The defendants placed advertisements in a Czech newspaper soliciting women to work in legitimate jobs in the United States. Upon arrival in the US the women found out the legitimate jobs did not exist, and they were forced to work in New York City strip clubs where customers fondled them for a fee.

Confinement: The women's passports were taken and they were not free to leave until they had paid off their smuggling debt.

Outcome: Both defendants received sentences of approximately five years incarceration for trafficking women into the US for prostitution or other immoral purposes, with two additional defendants being charged with witness tampering.

U.S. v. ZHENG QIAOCHHAI, ZHENG QIOYU, AND LIN XIAO 1998

Background: The defendants recruited women in China for jobs as waitresses in the Commonwealth of the Northern Marianas Islands in the District of

Guam. Shortly after the women arrived and started working in the bar, they were pressed into service as prostitutes.

Outcome: The defendants were convicted of two counts of conspiracy and transporting women in foreign commerce for purposes of prostitution by a jury in Saipan.

U.S. V. PAOLETTI 1997

Background: Since the early 1990s, the Paoletti family is believed to have trafficked over 1,000 deaf and mute Mexican women and men. The Mexicans were brought to the United States believing they would have good jobs. Once they arrived, they were forced to hawk trinkets and beg on subways and buses. They had a daily quota, and were beaten or mistreated if they did not make their quota.

Confinement: They were held under slave-like conditions, and not allowed to return to Mexico. The Paolettis held their documents under lock and key. Those who tried to leave were hunted down and returned to the workhouses. They were punished with beatings, forced menial labor, and constant supervision. In a few instances, stun guns were used on the victims as a form of punishment.

Outcome: Some 70 deaf Mexicans were found during a raid. In New York, a total of 20 persons were indicted on charges of: aiding and abetting; conspiracy; the bringing in, transporting, harboring, and inducement to enter of illegal aliens; the interference of commerce by threats or violence; and involuntary servitude. Eighteen pled guilty to their respective indictments. Adriana Lemus, the ringleader, received 14 years in prison, with the other co-conspirators receiving 1-to-8 year sentences depending on their involvement in the criminal scheme. In Charlotte, two defendants in the case pled guilty to aiding and abetting; conspiracy; and the bringing in, transporting, harboring and inducement to enter of illegal aliens. One defendant received a prison term of almost four years, the other received three years and four months. It is estimated that the Paoletti family made some $8 million dollars before they were arrested, and the judge ordered $1 million dollars in restitution in October 1998.

U.S. v. Wattanasiri 1995

Background: In conjunction with Thai traffickers, Ludwig Janak, a German national who operated a tour guide service in Thailand, recruited Thai women to come to the United States to work. Several of the women were told they would have good jobs working in restaurants. Once in the US, Thai traffickers and a Korean madam forced the women into prostitution.

Confinement: The women were held against their will at a brothel house and forced to work as prostitutes until their $35,000 smuggling debt was paid off. The women were kept in the underground brothel by bars on the windows and 24-hour surveillance. The defendants required that each woman sleep with four to five hundred customers to pay off the smuggling fee.

Outcome: A total of 18 defendants were indicted on

charges of kidnapping, alien smuggling, extortion, and white slavery. Twelve defendants were successfully prosecuted; the rest had fled to Thailand. Thus far, only two have been extradited from Thailand. The defendants were given sentences of between four and nine years.

U.S. v. MANASURANGKUN 1995

Background: Some seventy to seventy-eight Thai laborers, predominantly women from impoverished backgrounds with little education, were brought to the United States. The Thai traffickers promised the women high wages, good working hours, and freedom. Once they arrived in the United States, they were forced to labor in a sweatshop, working some 20-hour shifts in a garment factory.

Confinement: These Thai nationals were held against their will and systematically abused. The laborers were incarcerated in primitive conditions in a clandestine garment factory. High perimeter walls, razor wire, and corrugated steel panels were erected to conceal the facility. Additionally, around the clock sentries were installed to ensure no one escaped from the compound. The workers were made to pay an indentured servitude debt of between $8,000 and $15,000 and forced to write fake letters home, praising their working conditions.

Outcome: Seven defendants were convicted of alien smuggling, involuntary servitude, and civil rights violations. They received sentences ranging from four to seven years, with one defendant receiving seven months. Restitution in the amount of $4.5 million was ordered for the victims. Two additional defendants remain fugitives.

WHY WOMEN ARE TRAFFICKED TO THE UNITED STATES*

Prostitution

Latin America: (Mexican victims)
U.S. v. Cadena 1998

Asia: (Chinese-Korean victims)
U.S. v. Kwon 1998

Asia: (Korean, Mexican, and Thai vic-tims)
U.S. v. Kim, Phan, and Ortiz 1998

Asia: (Chinese victims)
U.S. v. Zheng Qiaochhai, Zheng Qioyu, Lin Xiao 1998

Asia: (Chinese victim)
U.S. v. Can 1997

Asia: (Thai victims) US v. Wattanasiri 1995

Asia: (Thai, Malaysian, and Singaporean victims)
Operation Ling 1997

Stripping/Sexual Touching

NIS: (Latvian victims)
U.S. v. Mishulovich 1999

Central Europe: (Czech Republic victims)
U.S. v. Lejhanec and Ruc 1998

Sweatshop Labor

Asia: (Chinese victims)
AFL-CIO, Global Exchange, Sweatshop Watch, Union of Needletrades Industrial and Textile Employees, and Asian Law Caucus. v. The Gap, The Associated Merchandising Corp., Cutter and Buck, Inc, Dayton-Hudson Corp., The Dress Barn, The Gymboree Corp., J.C. Penney Com-pany, J.Crew Group, Jones Apparel Group, Lady Bryant, The Limited, The May Department, Nordstrom, Oshkosh B_Gosh, Sears Roebuck and Company, Tommy Hilfiger, Wal-Mart, Warnaco Group, and Does 1-400 1999

Asia: (Thai victims)
U.S. v. Manasurangkun 1995 Agricultural Slave Labor

Latin America: (Mexican victims)
U.S. v. Cuello 1999

Latin America: (Mexican and Guatema-lan victims)
U.S. v. Flores 1997

Domestic Servitude

India: (Indian victim)
U.S. v. Mahtani 1996

Middle East: (Sri Lankan victim)
U.S. v. Alzanki 1995

Latin America: (Mexican victim)
U.S. v. Vargas 1991

Other Servitude

Latin America: (Mexican victims)
U.S. v. Lozano 1998

Latin America: (Mexican victims)
U.S. v. Paoletti 1997

*This is not an exhaustive list of all of the trafficking and slavery cases, but it does represent some of the more prominent and recent cases, and it exemplifies the various reasons why women are trafficked to the United States.

CHARACTERIZATION OF THE TRAFFICKERS IN THE UNITED STATES

In the United States, trafficking in women and children is primarily being conducted by smaller crime rings and loosely connected criminal networks. The nucleus of several of these crime rings centers around a family. There may be additional overlaps among the categories as many crime rings use their connections abroad to contract out duties. It is this amorphous nature of these rings and networks that make combating trafficking in women a challenging problem for law enforcement.

Small Crime Rings

Operation Ling
U.S. v. Cadena
U.S. v. Mishulovich
U.S. v. Ruc

Family Crime Rings

U.S. v. Can
U.S. v. Kwon
U.S. v. Lozano
U.S. v. Mahtani
U.S. v. Paoletti

Loosely Connected Criminal Networks

Project Orphan
U.S. v. Manasurangkun
U.S. v. Wattanasiri

Gangs

• Hmong case, Fresno-based gang involved in internal trafficking in California.

• Flying Dragons, a Chinese street gang that has provided protection to brothels where trafficking is thought to have occurred. The Flying Dragons is considered the enforcement sector of the HipsingTriad, a Fukienese Triad.

• Black Dragons and Koolboyz, Asian street gangs that have provided protection to brothels where trafficking is also thought to have occurred.

Note: The following Asian criminal organizations<the Sun Yee On Triad, 14K Triad, Wo Hop To Triad, the United Bamboo Gang, and Fuk Ching Gang<are involved in alien smuggling to the United States and it is likely that their activities include trafficking. The following major Russian organized crime syndicates (the Izmailovskaya, Dagestantsy, Kazanskaya, and Solntsenskaya) are involved in the prostitution industry throughout the United States. Given the way these

organized crime syndicates operate overseas and the brutality of these organizations, it is likely that this involvement in the US includes trafficking in women through the use of deception, threats, and violence.

GENERAL TIME SPAN OF THE TRAFFICKING OPERATIONS

A review of trafficking and slavery operations, involving sweatshop, agricultural, and other forms of labor, over the last eight years showed that these operations went unnoticed or were able to exist longer than sex trafficking operations. Labor trafficking operations generally lasted from four to six years, whereas trafficking operations for prostitution lasted from a little over a year to approximately two years before being discovered. Trafficking operations for other forms of the sex industry, such as exotic dancing and peep and touch shows, were in existence for anywhere from ten months to three years. Once uncovered, trafficking and slavery cases usually take about a year and a half to investigate and prosecute, according to the Department of Justice_s Involuntary Servitude Coordinator in the Civil Rights Division, Criminal Section.

The following is a list of cases and the length of time taken to discover, investigate, and prosecute.

- U.S. v. Wattanasiri: January 1994 – March 1995 (one year and about three months).

- U.S. v. Can: Beginning on or about September 24, 1994 to about April 19, 1996 (one year and seven months or so).

- U.S. v. Kwon: June 1995 to about January 1998 (two

years and seven months).

- U.S. v. Cadena: February 1996 to March 1998 (two years and one month).

- U.S. v. Mishulovich: October 1996 to about August 1997 (ten months).

- U.S. v. Ruc: Mid-1995 to about July 6, 1998 (about three years).

- U.S. v. Manasurangkun: From about April 1989 to about August 2, 1995 (six years and four months).

- CNMI labor suit: 1993 to the present (six years).

- U.S. v. Flores: From the late 1980s to fall 1996 (more than six years).

- U.S. v. Mahtani: Early 1995 to February 8, 1996 (roughly one year, one month).

- U.S. v. Paoletti: From approximately January 1993 to about July 1997 (four years and six months).

- U.S. v. Lozano: From about June 1992 to about 1998 (six years).

ROUTES TO AND WITHIN THE UNITED STATES:

- U.S. v. Wattanasiri: Bangkok to Bowery area of New York City, New York. Staging areas: Connecticut, Brooklyn, and Chinatown. Women also sent to: San Francisco, Dallas, Charlotte, and Kentucky.

- U.S. v. Can: PRC to Mexico to Washington, DC to New York to Los Angeles, California.

- U.S. v. Kwon: PRC to Saipan, Commonwealth of the Northern Mariana Islands (CNMI).

- U.S. v. Cadena: Veracruz state, Mexico to Houston, Texas to Florida. Once in Florida, the women and girls were rotated among brothels in the following Florida cities: Avon Park, Ft. Myers, Ft. Pierce, Haines City, Lake Worth, Okeechobee, Ocoee, Orlando, Tampa, and Zolfo Springs. They were also rotated between Lake City and John_s Island in South Carolina.

- U.S. v. Mishulovich: Riga, Latvia to Chicago, Illinois. Defendants also tried to recruit women in Minsk, Belarus.

- U.S. v. Ruc: Prague, Czech Republic to Brooklyn and New York City, New York.

- U.S. v. Manasurangkun: Bangkok, Thailand to Los Angeles, California to El Monte, California.

- U.S. v. Paoletti: Mexico to California to Los Angeles to Queens, New York and Chicago, Illinois. The Mexican victims were also transported to Boston, Massachusetts, Washington, DC, Baltimore, Maryland, Los Angeles, California, and Philadelphia, Pennsylvania, Sanford, North Carolina.

- U.S. v. Lozano: Mexico to El Paso, Texas and elsewhere in the US, including Albuquerque, New Mexico. The victims were transported among various cities including but not limited to Sanford, North

Carolina, Los Angeles, California, Albuquerque, New Mexico, Tucson, Arizona, and Phoenix, Arizona.

- U.S. v. Flores: Chandler Heights, Arizona at the US/Mexico border to Clarendon County, South Carolina.

- U.S. v. Mahtani: Bombay, India to Florida.

- U.S. v. Alzanki: Kuwait to Quincy, Massachusetts.

B1 (BUSINESS) AND B2 (TOURISM) VISA TIME LENGTH FROM MAJOR SOURCE COUNTRIES TO THE UNITED STATES

Russia
Multiple-entry visa valid for up to twelve months: $150
Multiple-entry visa valid for up to thirty-six months: $450

Ukraine
One entry valid for up to six months: $30
Two entries valid for up to six months: $60
Multiple-entry valid for up to thirty-six months: $120

Latvia
Multiple-entry valid for up to 120 months: no fee

The Czech Republic
Multiple-entry valid for up to 120 months: no fee

Poland
Multiple-entry valid for up to 120 months: no fee

Thailand
Multiple-entry valid for up to for 120 months: no fee

The Philippines
Multiple-entry valid for up to 120 months: no fee

China
Multiple-entry valid for up to six months: nofee

Mexico
Multiple-entry valid for up to 120 months: no fee

Note: Citizens wishing to travel to the United States from any of these countries, including those which say no fee, must pay an additional $45. This fee covers the costs associated with the machine-readable visa equipment. Information from the Department of State, Bureau of Consular Affairs, Visa Office.

International Trafficking in Women to the United States: A Contemporary Manifestation of Slavery and Organized Crime by Amy O'Neill Richard.

DCI Exceptional Intelligence Analyst Program, An Intelligence Monograph, Center for the Study of Intelligence, Central Intelligence Agency, Langley, VA, November 1999 (published April 2000)

Appendix II

International Organized Crime and its Involvement in Trafficking Women and Children Abroad

A review of US embassy, press, and non-governmental reports show that international criminal organizations are much more heavily involved in trafficking in women and children overseas than they are in the United States. The international trafficking trade appears to be highly organized, involving sophisticated international networks of procurers, document forgers and providers, escorts, organizers, financiers, corrupt officials, and brothel operators. International organized crime has capitalized on weak economies, corruption, and improved international transportation infrastructure to traffic some 700,000 to two million women and children globally each year. Southeast Asia comprises nearly one-third of this global trade. The Newly Independent States and Eastern Europe have risen to roughly one-fourth of the world_s trade, making it one of the faster growing regions in the world.141 The number of organized crime groups engaged in trafficking is likely to continue increasing, given the high profit potential and relatively low penalties.

Asian Organized Crime

On April 23 1999, ministers from eighteen Asia-Pacific countries issued the Bangkok declaration stating that they are gravely concerned by the increasing activities of transnational organized criminal groups who are profiting from trafficking in human beings, especially women and children. They also said that the participating countries should be encouraged to pass legislation to criminalize trafficking in human beings, especially women and children, in all its forms and purposes, including as sources of cheap labor. They called for countries to cooperate as necessary in the prosecution and penalization of all offenders, especially international organized criminal groups.

Regional destination countries, such as Australia, have noticed a rise in women trafficked to their countries and the involvement of organized crime in the industry. Australia_s Justice Minister stated last year that there had been a noticeable increase in the number of Asian women lured to Australia with the pretense of legitimate jobs only to find themselves working in virtual slavery in legal and illegal brothels. International crime syndicates, some with links to the drug trade, are arranging the women_s movement.143 The American consulate in Sydney reports that Southeast Asian women are being trafficked to Australia by international organized crime syndicates, such as the 14K, a Chinese triad. There is evidence of organized crime groups making multi-million-dollar profits from prostitution, much of it untaxed and moved offshore.

The Triads

Major Asian organized crime groups are involved in trafficking women and children. In China, the Sun Yee On, 14 K, Big Circle Boys, and Wo On Lok Triads have all repeatedly been linked to smuggling illegal immigrants and prostitution rackets. The American Embassy in London reports that Chinese Triads are the primary traffickers of women and girls from Southeast Asia, South America, and Eastern Europe to Britian. Press reports indicate that Chinese Triads have also worked with Russian organized crime groups in trafficking. Upon arrival, the victims are held prisoner until further money is paid or they are forced into bonded labor, such as sweatshops or prostitution. Italian prosecutors maintain that Chinese, Albanian, and Nigerian crime groups dominate the trafficking and slave trade in Italy, with the Chinese largely involved in slave labor. Thirty-three members of the Serpents Head—the Milan cell of the Grand Dragon Triad—were sentenced in Italy in September 1998 for trafficking. Malaysian police and non-governmental organizations believe that ethnic Chinese criminal syndicates are behind most of the trafficking in their country. Trafficked women are usually fed into an extensive system of Chinese owned lounges, nightclubs, and brothels that exist throughout much of Asia. Chinese criminal organizations have also been involved in abducting and selling women and children in China itself. For example, the Song clan group in Lixin county in Anhui set up special operations in Chengdu under the guise of hiring people to go to Shanghai to get apparel or go to Anhui to purchase traditional Chinese medicines. Lured under false pretenses, the young women were then kidnapped and delivered to buyers.

The Yakuza

The American Embassy in Tokyo reports that Japanese organized crime or the Yakuza are involved in trafficking in women and the adult entertainment industry. Local brokers approach women in their home country and offer well-paying jobs in legitimate professions abroad. Once in Japan, they are funneled to their actual employers by intermediaries, primarily Japanese, who often have purchased the rights to these women from the source country brokers. The usual pay for these women is 2 million yen or approximately $14,000 to $15,000 at 1998 exchange rates. According to a Wellesley College professor who is researching trafficking in women and traveled to Japan last spring, the Yakuza have increasingly become involved in the trafficking of persons since the bubble economy burst in 1992 and they had to look for additional means of income. She reports that the Yakuza view trafficking in women as a business and protect their "investment" by detailing a "bodyguard" to monitor the movements of each woman or girl. They will post pictures of a woman or girl who has escaped, and encourage members or affiliates to turn her in if found. This professor claims that corruption is a problem as the police are often the ones who turn the escapee in to the mob. The U.S. Legal Attaché serving in Manila reports that those Filipinas who have tried to flee in Japan have been killed. Non-governmental organizations also claim that several shelters for escapees had been vandalized severely by the Yakuza in the last few years. Subsequently, the shelters changed locations and now operate under cover. The Japanese National Police Agency concurs that there has been a rise in foreigners forced into prostitution in Japan. The women, mostly from Asia and Latin America, are commonly recruited to be bar hostesses, but on arrival are forced into prostitution. They are kept under constant surveillance and all earnings are turned over to the traffickers.149 Investigations by the non-governmental organization Global Survival Network, reveal that the Japanese Yakuza are involved in the trafficking industry, often in cooperation with the Russian mafia. The Yakuza not only force Russian women, who thought they were going to work in Japan as hostesses, into prostitution but also traffic Thai and Mexican women to Japanese brothels. The Thai women are frequently bought from Thai traffickers, while the Mexican women are duped into thinking they would be singers or actresses in Japan. The Yakuza have also been known to traffic women from the United States to Japan.

The Yakuza also work with Filipino recruiters to traffic Filipina women to Hong Kong and Japan, according to the legal attaché in Manila. The Yakuza use local illegal recruiters to get the women to go to Japan to work as bar hostesses, but many are then forced into prostitution. Batis, a Manila non-governmental organization, agrees that the Yakuza are working with local recruiters in Manila. Batis reports that a variety of sex establishments are owned by the Yakuza in the Philippines and in Japan. Women are held in these clubs in Japan under the supervision of the Yakuza. A recruiter gets paid $6,000 to $10,000 per woman he recruits to go to Japan. The club then pays the recruiter. Batis claims that the recruiter often targets the most vulnerable women, usually those from the areas that have been destroyed by typhoons.

Thai Criminal Networks

Besides the Triads and the Yakuza, Thai criminal networks are involved in trafficking in women. Law enforcement reports that there are at least seven "families" in Bangkok, Thailand who recruit, sell, and smuggle Asian women throughout the world, including the U.S., to serve as prostitutes. These families secure identity/travel documents, arrange travel itineraries, and then broker the women to agents representing brothels in the U.S., Japan, Canada, and Australia. The agents charge the women roughly $40,000 to effect entry into the U.S. Upon entry, the agent is responsible for paying a fee to the smuggling organization in Thailand. The female_s debt is repaid by her engagement in prostitution. Until the payment is made, the woman is under the control of the agent and is frequently sold, battered, or exchanged. The women are smuggled into a foreign country utilizing photo-substituted or impostor Thai passports. After arrival the passports are usually returned to the smuggler in Thailand and recycled. The Thai smugglers use escorts called _jockeys_ to transport the females to the US. The jockey is paid $1,000 per person for the trip. He assists in getting the non-English speaking women through the INS and Customs inspection process. After clearing Customs, the jockey delivers the women to the domestic agent who will then place her with the brothel.

Russian Organized Crime

Russian organized crime's traditional involvement in prostitution has grown to include trafficking. Russian organized crime provides "the roof," or cover for trafficking operations, while lower-level Russian criminals manage recruitment and logistics. Russian criminals often operate behind the facades of employment, travel, modeling, and/or matchmaking agencies. The Global Survival Network concurs that traffickers use matchmaking or marriage agency databases to identify women looking for a better life abroad. Another American non-governmental organization, MiraMed, says traffickers in Russia have gone so far as to set up "career day" booths in institutes and universities, promising profitable work abroad. Traffickers often provide women with counterfeit travel documents or assist them in obtaining genuine documents through fraud. Russian organized crime groups are reportedly cooperating with Albanian, Turkish, former Yugoslavian crime groups, Chinese Triads, and the Japanese Yakuza to traffic women to Western Europe and Japan.

The International Organization for Migration and the Global Survival Network report that Russian organized crime groups control European prostitution industries, such as those in Poland, Germany, and Italy. Bulgarian Interior Ministry Chief Secretary Bozhidar Popov has also said that Russian criminals are trafficking Russian, Ukrainian, Georgian, and Chechen women through Bulgaria to Turkey, Greece and elsewhere in Western Europe for prostitution. One major Russian criminal syndicate, the Mogilevich organization, owns night clubs in Prague, Riga, and Kiev and has engaged in trafficking in women for forced prostitution at these clubs. The powerful Ismailovskaya syndicate is under intense investigation by a variety of European law enforcement structures for involvement in trafficking in women and children as well as drug trafficking and counterfeit cigarette manufacturing. Lithuanian Member of Parliament Vilija Aleknaite-Abramikiene reports that Russian organized crime groups are heavily involved in trafficking women for the sex industry in Lithuania. In Russia's Far East, Russian criminals reportedly supplied Russian women to brothels and clubs in Hong Kong and Macao. Commander Ina Volf of the Israeli national police believes that Russian organized crime is involved in trafficking from the Newly Independent States. A report by Israel's Women's Network found that Russian organized crime controls the sex industry throughout Israel. There are roughly nine to ten Russian prostitution rings operating in Israel. Territory has been divided among the crime bosses. It has become a whole industry; recruiting the women, bringing them to Israel, and distributing them to the various brothels. Knesset member Marina Solodkin claims that local Israeli mafioso are also involved in the trafficking industry.

Israel's Women's Network also reports that a protection racket has grown up around the trafficking and prostitution business in Israel. There is a symbiotic relationship between the police and pimps in which pimps may provide useful intelligence to police on criminal activity in Israel. The police see them as valuable sources of information and work to turn the pimps into collaborators. Overall, trafficking and prostitution is a lucrative business in Israel where Soviet-immigrant Israeli bosses make anywhere from $1,000 to $4,000 a day off the women.

Elsewhere in the Middle East, police and other sources in the United Arab Emirates generally believe that crime organizations from Russia and the Newly Independent States are involved in local prostitution involving women from their countries, according to the American Embassy in Dubai.

Besides Europe, Asia, and the Middle East, Russian organized crime is involved in trafficking women to Canada, according to the American Embassy in Toronto. Russian criminals ran a trafficking ring in 1991 in Canada involving eleven women from the Newly Independent States. The women came to work as models but were compelled to become strippers. They were forced to turn over their return airline tickets, passports, and cash for "safekeeping." Their handlers also reportedly kept them confined and forced them to turn over their earnings. They were made them to comply by threats of death and bodily harm to their loved ones in the Newly Independent States. Russian organized criminals have also been involved in extortion from women who have tried to come forward to prosecute their traffickers.

Ukrainian Criminal Syndicates

Ukrainian organized crime groups are heavily involved in trafficking of women, according to the American Embassy in Kiev. Organized crime syndicates bribe Ukrainian immigration officials to look the other way, or in some cases, to facilitate the illegal entry or exit of undocumented or improperly documented women. The International Organization for Migration reports that the majority of young Ukrainian women and girls are first recruited for ostensibly legal, mainly unskilled jobs before being forced into the sex business. The majority of the recruiters, who initiate the first contact with the victims, are young males between the ages of 20 and 25 years old. The recruiters are usually friends or acquaintances, or have made considerable efforts to gain their trust. Ukrainian crime groups reportedly control the prostitution markets in Hungary and Austria. A Ukrainian mafia boss was arrested in June 1997 at the Austrian/Italian border at Tarvisio. In cooperation with Albanian criminals, he had been trafficking dozens of Ukrainian girls to Italy and forcing them into prostitution.159 The American Embassy in Ankara reports that there are allegations that the Ukrainian mafia is turning women over to the Turkish mafia for $2,000 to $3,000 a woman.

Georgian Crime Groups

The American Embassy in T'bilisi reports that Georgian trafficking rings with strong ties to Russian organized crime traffic women through employment agencies used as fronts. Some rings specialize in trafficking women for the sex industry while others concentrate on labor exploitation. These organized rings traffic young women, between the ages of sixteen and thirty, to the United States for prostitution, while older women, forty-five and older, may be trafficked for indentured servitude. The older women are aware they will be working as maids and nannies but unaware that they will be doing it for virtually no remuneration. The traffickers often supply the victims with counterfeit documents to obtain genuine visas and arrange for their travel to the U.S. Someone from the trafficking organization will meet them upon arrival at an U.S. airport and confiscate their passports, stranding them in the United States. Next, the women are placed in strip clubs, massage parlors, brothels, or households. They are expected to repay the traffickers for living expenses, transportation costs to the US, the costs of obtaining fraudulent documents, plus a penalizing interest on their debt. These women become in effect indentured servants, bound to work for free until their debts to the traffickers are repaid.

Polish Crime Groups

In addition to being a source country, Poland is a transit country for women trafficked from other countries, such as Bulgaria, Romania and the Newly Independent States. The American Embassy in Warsaw reports that Polish criminal networks recruit, transport, and deliver women from these countries into the hands of organized prostitution rings in destination countries. They may sell these women for about $30,000 each to Vietnamese, Ukrainian, Armenian, and Turkish gangs that dominate prostitution markets in Germany and other Western European countries. The new owners confiscate the women's travel documents and use beatings, gang rapes, and drugs to force them into prostitution. The women become virtual prisoners in the brothels, and are required to serve 10 to 20 clients a day. There is also a growing tendency for victims to be drugged and kidnapped from public places, such as discos or pubs.162 In Spain, Polish and Czech organized crime groups operate under the guise of travel agencies, according to the American Embassy in Madrid. They recruit the women and deliver them to their new handlers in Spain but are not involved in local prostitution. They use the threat of arrest and deportation to control the women.

Trafficking is also an efficiently cruel enterprise in Poland, which is increasingly becoming a destination country. Once the women and girls are brought to Poland, traffickers take away their passports and force them into prostitution to work off their debts and earn back their travel documents. Girls who resist are raped, beaten, or confined with minimal food and water until they comply. In some cases, girls have been killed for resisting trafficker's demands. Traffickers sink profits from their prostitution rings into illegal narcotics, weapons, or stolen cars.

Many trafficking and prostitution enterprises are conducted by small organized rings of five to six persons, with criminal contacts. In some cases, these small rings are operated on the side by bigger trafficking rings. Generally, traffickers in both the origin and destination country have links to professional criminal organizations, which provide protection for the trafficker and brothels, and are used to intimidate the women. Many of the recruiters, who form the first contact with the victims, are young males between twenty and twenty-five years old, while the trafficker who runs the operation is generally between twenty and fifty-five years old.

Albanian Crime Groups

Albanian criminal groups are rapidly expanding their organized drug networks to include prostitution rings that operate in northern Italy. The Executive Director of UNICEF, Carol Bellamy, says there is growing evidence of trafficking in girls from Albania to Italy. Criminal clans, often based on family ties, target orphans and young girls from large families in Albania and lure them abroad with promises of marriage and/or jobs as waitresses or domestics. The American Consulate in Milan reports that a recent development is the increase in trafficking of minors, primarily Albanians, spawned by the hope that young girls are free of AIDs. Typically, the criminals smuggle the girls by rubber dinghy from Valona in southern Albania to Puglia in southern Italy. From there, they transport them to northern Italy via taxi, train, or semi-trucks.

Albanian criminals are also taking advantage of broken-up families and confusion in the refugee camps in neighboring countries to target and traffic Kosovo minors for adoption or the sex industry.167 Girls have ended up in prostitution and child exploitation rings in northern Italy, especially Turin and Milan. The American Consulate in Milan also reports that there is growing evidence of torture and terror by the Albanian criminals in order to keep these girls in line. Uncooperative girls have been killed. Dr. Pier Luigi Vigna, Italy's National Anti-Mafia Prosecutor, concurs about the extreme violence of the Albanian crime groups, noting a case where Albanian girls were tattooed with the crime group's symbols. In other cases, the Albanians have burned their victims for punishment.

General Francesco Saverio Polella, head of the National Investigation Division of Italy's Anti-Mafia Directorate, said in July that Albanian and Italian crime groups are cooperating in transporting drugs and trafficking women and girls into Italy. Once in Italy, the Albanians are managing the selling of the women and girls into prostitution. One Albanian women's organization concluded in a study that Albanian gangs sell the girls to criminal organizations in Italy and/or Greece for $10,000. To facilitate their business and these transactions, Mr. Polella also claims that the Albanian crime groups have divided up specific tasks, such as recruitment, transportation, and prostitution, amongst themselves in their trafficking operations. Some experts claim that Albanian criminal organizations are also recruiting directly in Belgian refugee centers. Albanian criminal groups are taking control of prostitution networks in Belgium, particularly Antwerp and Brussels. These gangs have now established territorial control of the streets and districts where they are free to develop other criminal activities, such as drug trafficking and racketeering. Girls brought to Belgium by other criminal organizations are being "stolen" from them by the Albanians. By some accounts, the Albanians are believed to be working as subcontractors for the Turkish mafia, whose members are increasingly distancing themselves from the operational level, for heroin trafficking. The traditional intermediaries, previously French, Moroccans and Turks, have been supplanted by Albanians, either from Albania or Kosovo.

Nigerian Crime Rings

The American Embassy in Lagos reports that trafficking in women tends to be more of a localized cottage industry than an organized racket involving

Nigerian criminal syndicates. Italian prosecutors believe that Nigerian rings are trafficking women to and within Italy for the sex industry. The American Consulate in Milan reports that a Nigerian slave trade operates in Genoa, Italy. Nigerian women and men have been involved in abetting illegal immigration, reducing girls to slavery, forcing them into prostitution, and exploiting them for profit. Girls from Africa are lured to Italy with promises of work as bar girls, waitresses, or models. They are then forced upon arrival to undress and promenade nude before fellow Nigerians who pay $9,000 to $30,000 depending on the girls' age and physical attributes. The women and girls are kept in submission by threats, voodoo, and magic. In Naples, Italy's National Anti-Mafia Prosecutor said in July that the Camorra, an Italian organized crime group, rent streets to Nigerians whom have trafficked Nigerian women to Italy for prostitution. In Spain, the American Embassy in Madrid reports that the African trafficking rings are the least organized and sophisticated of the trafficking organizations operating there. They rely on force to maintain discipline.

International Trafficking in Women to the United States: A Contemporary Manifestation of Slavery and Organized Crime by Amy O'Neill Richard.

DCI Exceptional Intelligence Analyst Program, An Intelligence Monograph, Center for the Study of Intelligence, Central Intelligence Agency, Langley, VA, November 1999 (published April 2000).

NOTES

PROLOGUE

"We're talking about . . . Carol Bellamy, 10 Million Children Exploited For Domestic Labor, June 14, 2004.

CHAPTER 1: HUMAN TRAFFICKING

She was a normal . . . Anna Dolgov, Associated Press, Russian Women Fight Sex Trafficking, 5/16/01.

"There were fines for everything; . . . Anna Dolgov, Associated Press, Russian Women Fight Sex Trafficking, 5/16/01.

Siri started out in life . . . Kevin Bales, *Disposable People: New Slavery in the Global Economy*, University of California Press, Berkeley, California, 1999.

As a punishment for . . . Kevin Bales, *Disposable People: New Slavery in the Global Economy*, University of California Press, Berkeley, California, 1999.

The Cadenas would then . . . Florida State University Center for Advancement of Human Rights, Trafficking Cases in Florida, *Florida Responds to Human Trafficking*.

When Anastasia disappeared . . . David Fisher, *Seattle Post-Intelligencer*, Indle King found guilty of killing mail-order bride, 2/22/02.

As I learned . . . Congresswoman Louise M. Slaughter (N.Y.) in support of the Smith-Morella-Slaughter-Lantos-Pitts amendment to the Foreign Operations appropriations bill (H.R. 2506), July 24, 2001.

Human trafficking today . . . Senator Sam Brownbeck (KS), in a press conference and release on September 23, 2003.

In the Commonwealth . . . Statement of U.S. Senator Daniel K. Akaka, Human Trafficking for Forced Labor in an American Commonwealth, May 26, 1999.

A man and his wife . . . George Christopoulos, Family Ran Prostitution Ring, *Toronto Sun*, May 16, 1998.

"Sadly, many people have . . . Canadian Department of Justice report, "Trafficking in Persons," April 23, 2004.

"I am pleased . . . Irwin Cotler, Minister of Justice and Attorney General of Canada, "Forum on Human Trafficking," Ottawa, Ontario, March 30, 2004.

"If Tony Blair . . . Ros Coward, Slaves in Soho, *The Guardian*, March 26, 2003.

"Criminals who smuggle aliens . . . Statement of U.S. Attorney Roslynn Mauskopf to *Newsday* writer Robert E. Kessler, 6/22/04.

"Up to 10 million children . . . United Nations press release, 10 Million Children Exploited for Domestic Labor, June 14, 2004.

"They may be burned or otherwise tortured . . . Dr. June Kane, Helping Hands or Shackled Lives, ILO, CH-1211 Geneva 22, Switzerland, 2004.

CHAPTER 2: NEW SLAVE TRADERS

"I was told that I would . . . Zaklina Gorgevik, *Utrinski Vesnik*, 2/18/03.

In his book, The Natashas . . . Victor Malarek, *The Natashas: The New Global Sex Trade*, Viking, Canada, 2003.

To their horror . . . Victor Malarek, *The Natashas: The New Global Sex Trade*, Viking, Canada, 2003.

They all operate . . . Amy O'Neill Richards, U.S. State Department's Bureau of Intelligence and Research Report, *International Trafficking in Women to the United States: A Contemporary Manifestation of Slavery and Organized Crime*, 11/99.

According to the Congressional . . . Francis T. Miko, Congressional Research Service report for Congress, *Trafficking in Women and Children: The U.S. and International Response*, 3/26/04.

"At the center of . . . Thomas Zambito, "From Russia as 'Slaves,'" *New York Daily News*, 6/14/04.

CHAPTER 3: ANCIENT SLAVERY

There are prehistoric . . . Hugh Thomas, *Slave Trade*, Simon & Schuster, 1997.

Tertullian wrote that . . . *On the Public Shows* qtd. in Mattingly.

CHAPTER 4: BREAKING THE NEW SLAVE TRADE

In the last three . . . Donna M. Hughes, Ph.D. Professor and Carlson Endowed Chair in Women's Studies at the University of Rhode Island, "Trafficking of Women and Children in East Asia and Beyond: A Review of U.S. Policy" Subcommittee of East Asian and Pacific Affairs Senate Foreign Relations Committee, April 9, 2003.

CONCLUSION

For example, according . . . Amy O'Neill Richard, U.S. State Department's Bureau of Intelligence and Research Report, *International Trafficking in Women to the United States: A Contemporary Manifestation of Slavery and Organized Crime*, 11/99.

BIBLIOGRAPHY

Cases (Indictments, Affidavits)

U.S. v. Bonds, Indictment, CR 93, U.S. District Court for the Eastern District of North Carolina, Raleigh Division.

U.S. v. Cadena, Superseding Indictment, Case No. 98-14015-CR-RYSKAMP, U.S. District Court, Southern District of Florida, April 23, 1998; Videotaped deposition of a victim, November 5, 1998; Victim Impact Letters.

U.S. v. Cam, U.S. District Court for the Central District of California, CR 96-459, June 1995.

U.S. v. Cortez, Indictment, 2:97-560, U.S. District Court of South Carolina, Charleston Division, June 18, 1997.

U.S. v. Driggers, 2:97, U.S. District Court of South Carolina, Charleston Division, May 8, 1997.

U.S. v. Flores, Indictment, 2:96-806, U.S. District Court of South Carolina, Charleston Division, October 10, 1996.

U.S. v. Kwon, Indictment, U.S. District Court for the Northern Mariana Islands, CR 98-00044, November 1998.

U.S. v. Lozano, Indictment, EP 98 CR 0335, U.S. District Court for the Western District of Texas, El Paso Division, March 1998.

U.S. v. Manasurangkun, Superseding Indictment, CR 95-714 (A), U.S. District Court for the Central District of California, February 1995; Government_s Filing of the Original Executed Plea Agreement, CR 95-714 (B), U.S. District Court for the Central District of California, February 9, 1996.

U.S. v. Mishulovich, Superseding Indictment, U.S. District Court, Northern District of Illinois, Eastern Division, April 22, 1999; FBI Affidavit, September 9, 1998.

U.S. v. Paoletti, Indictment, CR 97 768, U.S. District Court Eastern District of New York, August 19, 1998; Superseding Information.

U.S. v. Ruc, Diplomatic Security, Criminal Intelligence Report, V-96-00098, March 1998.

U.S. v. Wattanasiri, Indictment, S.R. 95 Cr. 52, U.S. District Court, Southern District of New York.

U.S. v. Wuttidetgrienggrai, Indictment, 95 Cr. 200, U.S. District Court, Southern District of New York.

Class Action, AFL-CIO, Global Exchange, Sweatshop Watch, Union of Needletrades Industrial and Textile Employees, and Asian Law Caucus. v. The Gap, The Associated Merchandising Corp., Cutter and Buck, Inc., Dayton-Hudson Corp., The Dress Barn, The Gymboree Corp., J.C. Penney Company, J.Crew Group, Jones Apparel Group, Lady Bryant, The Limited, The May Department, Nordstrom, Oshkosh B_Gosh, Sears Roebuck and Company, Tommy Hilfiger, Wal-Mart, Warnaco Group, and Does 1-400, U.S. District Court for the Central District of California, 1999.

Dailies, Quarterlies

Department of Justice, Immigration and Naturalization Service, "Borderline," *Intelligence Daily Report*, September 1998, October 1999.

Department of State, Bureau of Consular Affairs Fraud Prevention Programs, Monthly Bulletins.

Gender Matters Quarterly, U.S.AID Office of Women in Development, Gender Research Project, "Women as Chattel: The Emerging Global Market in Trafficking," February 1999.

International Organization for Migration, Trafficking in Migrants, Quarterly Bulletins, September 1998-September 1999.

Interviews

(T) indicates the interview was a telephone interview. Otherwise, the interview occurred in person.

Department of Justice

Attorney General Janet Reno, September 1999.

Public Policy Office, November 1998.

Civil Rights Division, Criminal Section, October 1998, April, November 1999.

Child Exploitation Obscenity Section, September 1998, August 1999.

Office of International Affairs, November 1998.

Office for Victims of Crimes, January 1999.

Civil Rights Division, Office of Special Counsel for Immigration Related Unfair Employment Practices, March 1999.

National Central Bureau for Interpol, March 1999 (T).

DOJ worker abuse and exploitation one-day training course, Washington, DC, October 1998.

Assistant U.S. Attorney, Brooklyn, New York, December 1998.

Assistant U.S. Attorney, Los Angeles, California, February 1998.

Assistant U.S. Attorney, Miami, Florida, April 1999.

Assistant U.S. Attorney, Fort Lauderdale, Florida, May 1999 (T).

Assistant U.S. Attorney, New York, New York, May 1999.

Assistant U.S. Attorney, Chicago, Illinois, July 1999.

Legal Attachés, Asia, Bangkok, Thailand, February 1999.

Legal Attachés, Manila, Philippines, February 1999.

International Law Enforcement Academy Asia Director, Bangkok, Thailand, February 1999.

Federal Bureau of Investigation

Intelligence Research Office, September, October 1998.

FBI Agents, New York, December 1998.

FBI Agent, West Palm Beach, April 1999.

FBI Agent, Miami, August 1999 (T).

FBI Headquarters, October 1999.

Immigration and Naturalization Service

INS regional intelligence conference, New Orleans, Louisiana, September, 1999.

INS Intelligence Workshop at the Naval Academy, Annapolis, Maryland, March 1999.

INS Agent, Vancouver, Canada, August 1998.

INS, Smuggling Criminal Organizations Branch, October 1998.

INS Investigations, October 1998.

INS Investigations, Field Operations, July 1999 (T).

INS Agent, Louisville, Kentucky, October 1998 (T).

INS Agent, New Orleans, November 1998 (T).

INS Office of Detention and Deportation, November 1998.

INS Agents, New York City, December 1998.

INS Agents, Los Angeles, January 1999, September 1999 (T).

INS Bangkok, Thailand February 1999.

INS Manila, Philippines, February, 1999.

INS Agent, Los Angeles, February 1999.

INS, U.S. Border Patrol, Anti-Smuggling Unit, April 1999.

INS Agent, New York, May 1999.

INS Juvenile Coordinator, August 1999 (T).

U.S. Marshal Service

U.S. Marshal Service, Miami, Florida, May 1999 (T).

Drug Enforcement Agency

DEA country attaché, Manila, Philippines, February 1999.

Department of Labor

Wage and Hour Division, November 1999.

Department of State

Deputy Chief of Mission, Bangkok, Thailand, February, 1999.

Deputy Chief of Mission, Manila, Philippines, February 1999.

President's Interagency Council on Women (constant and ongoing contact), September 1998—October 1999.

Bureau of International Narcotics and Law Enforcement Affairs (constant and ongoing contact), September 1998—October 1999.

Bureau of Consular Affairs

Office of Fraud Prevention Program, November, December 1998.

Office of Visas, July 1999 (T).

Consular Affairs, Vancouver, August 1999.

Consular Affairs, Bangkok, Thailand, February 1999.

Consular Affairs, Manila, Philippines, February 1999.

Diplomatic Security

DS Agents, September, December, 1998, July 1999.

DS Agent, Miami, Florida, April 1999 (T).

Agency for International Development

USAID, Counselor, Manila, Philippines, February 1999.

AID anti-trafficking team for Asia, March 1999.

Department of Treasury

Customs officers, December 1998, January 1997.

State Police

Washington, D.C. Police Academy, one-day training course on the sex industry in the U.S. and child exploitation issues, November 1998.

Maryland State Trooper, March 1999.

New Jersey Law Enforcement, May 1999 (T).

Florida Law Enforcement, Panama City, May 1999 (T).

Intelligence Community

CIA Office of Transnational Issues, Crime and Narcotics Center.

NSA.

Non-governmental Organizations

Amnesty International officers, May 1999.

Asian Women Human Rights Council, Quezon City, Philippines, February 1999.

Batis Center for Women, Manila, Philippines, February 1999.

Center for the Pacific-Asian Family, Outreach to Trafficking Victims, Los Angeles, California, February 1999.

Coalition Against Trafficking Worldwide, New York, December 1998 Manila, Philippines, February 1999.

End Child Prostitution, Child Pornography, and Trafficking in Children, Washington, D.C., November 1999, Manila, Philippines, February 1999.

Florida Immigrant Advocacy Center, West Palm Beach, Florida, April 1999.

Global Survival Network, October 1998, April 1999, October 1999.

Helping Individual Prostitutes Survive, October 1998 (T).

Human Rights Watch, November 1998.

India-Canada Cooperation Center, New Delhi, January 1999.

International Human Rights Law Group, October 1998, November 1999.

International Labor Organization, International Program on the Elimination of Child Labor, Bangkok, Thailand, February 1999.

International Labor Rights Fund, October 1998.

International Organization for Migration (IOM), Washington, DC, October, 1998.

IOM, Bangkok, Thailand, February 1999.

IOM, Manila, Philippines, February 1999.

Legal Aid for Cambodia, November 1998.

Little Tokyo Service Center, Coalition to Abolish Slavery and Trafficking, Los Angeles, California, February 1999.

MiraMed Institute, November 1998, September 1999.

National Center for Missing and Exploited Children, October 1998.

OSCE, Office for Democratic Institutions and Human Rights, Poland, May 1999.

Philippines American Services Group, November 1998.

Philippine Network Against Trafficking of Women, Quezon City, Philippines, February 1999.

Visayan Foundation, Manila, Philippines, February 1999.

Women, Law, and Development, December 1998.

Academia

Dr. Louise Shelley, American University, Director, Transnational Crime and Corruption Center, and Dr. Sally Stoecker, Human Trafficking Director and Research Professor, American University, Transnational Crime and Corruption Center, May 1999.

Dr. Laura Lederer, Harvard University, The Protection Project, November 1998, July 1999.

Dr. Kathryn McMahon, California State University, Associate Director Southeast Asian Studies Center, Professor International Studies and Women's Studies, February 1999 (T).

Dr. Katharine Moon, Professor, Department of Political Science, Wellesley College, March 1999.

Foreign Government Officials

Vilija Aleknaite-Abramikiene, Lithuanian Member of Parliament, October 9, 1999.

Roundtable discussion in Vancouver, Canada on trafficking in women and children with representatives from the RCMP Criminal Investigations Unit, RCMP Immigration and Passport Section, RCMP General Investigation Section, British Columbia Ministry of the Attorney General, Canadian Citizenship and Immigration agency, August 1998.

Met with South Asian (Bangladesh, India, Nepal, and Pakistan) trafficking experts, Washington, D.C., September 1998.

Roundtable discussion with trafficking in women experts from Russia, March 1999.

Roundtable discussion with the Philippines Overseas Employment Administration, Filipino National Police Criminal Investigation Group, Philippine Anti-Organized Crime Task Force, Philippine Task Force on Illegal Recruitment, Manila, Philippines, February 1999.

Philippines Department of Foreign Affairs, Office of European Affairs, and ASEAN office, Manila, Philippines, February 1999.

Philippines Department of Justice, Bureau of Immigration, and Intelligence Division, Manila, Philippines, February 1999.

Commission on Filipinos Overseas, Manila, Philippines, February 1999.

The Netherlands, National Criminal Intelligence Division, Alien Smuggling Unit, Washington, D.C., April 1999.

Roundtable discussion, U.S./Italian Bilateral Working Group on Trafficking in Women, July 14-16, 1999.

Press

Agence France Presse, "Japan Reports Rise in Foreigners Forced Into Prostitution," April 6, 1998.

Agence France Presse, "Australia to Crack Down on Asian Sex Slaves," April 14, 1998.

Associated Press, "Indictment Charges 23 Hmongs with Series of Rapes," October 20, 1999.

Associated Press, "Police Bust California Sex-Slave Ring," November 19, 1998.

Associated Press, "Police Break Up Sex-Slave Ring That Preyed On Immigrant Girls," November 13, 1998.

Associated Press, "Two Plead Guilty in Mexican Baby Smuggling Case," July 15, 1999.

Associated Press, "Adoptions of Smuggled Mexican Babies," July 25, 1999.

Associated Press, "Prostitution Lord Admits Smuggling Mexican Women in the U.S. as Sex Slaves," January 19, 1999.

Associated Press, "Sisters Sentenced to Eight Years in Prison in Slave Labor Case," January 16, 1999.

Barry, John, *Miami Herald*, "Tortured Au Pair Finds A New Life," July 31, 1998.

Bennetto, Jason, "Triads Target British Sex Trade," *The Independent*, August 11, 1997.

Booth, William, "13 Charged in Gang Importing Prostitutes," *The Washington Post*, August 21, 1999.

Branigin, William, "Modern-Day Slavery? Imported Servants Allege Abuse By Foreign Host Families in U.S.," *The Washington Post*,

January 5, 1999.

Branigin, William, "A Life of Exhaustion, Beatings and Isolation," *The Washington Post*, January 1999.

Branigin, William, "Human Rights Group Urges Action on Saipan," *The Washington Post*, May 4, 1999.

"China: How Criminal Organizations Acquire Illicit Wealth," *Daily Report China*, August 12, 1997.

Johnston, Philip, "Triads and Mafia Cash In On Illegal Immigrants," *The Daily Telegraph*, November 27, 1997.

Kleinfield, N.R., "Five Charged With Holding Thai Women Captive for Prostitution," *The New York Times*, December 20, 1995

Korecki, Natasha, "FBI Breaks Crime Rink Linked to Russian Mafia," *Chicago Daily Herald*, September 19, 1998.

Lardner, George, "16 Charged With Forcing Mexicans Into Prostitution," *The Washington Post*, April 24, 1998.

Mercyhurst, "UN Representative to Travel to Guatemala to Assess Sale of Children," July 13, 1999.

"Haitian Girl Illegally Residing in the U.S., Sexually Abused and Forced to be a Maid," *Miami Herald*, September 30, 1999.

Navarro, Mireya, "Case of Florida Au Pair Reflects Wider Problem," *The New York Times*, December 12, 1998.

Nicholson, Kieran and Wheeler, Sheba, "Three Held in Alleged Sex Slave Ring," *Denver Post*, November 13, 1998.

Reuters, "Illegal Alien Heads Miami Forced Prostitution Ring," January 15, 1999.

Reuters, "UNHCR Chief Says Refugees Forced Into Prostitution," May 5, 1999.

Reuters, "UNICEF Sees Prostitution Among Kosovo Albanians," May 20, 1999.

Shroder, Lisa, "The Servant's Tale," *Sun-Sentinel*, November 12, 1998.

Smith, Stephanie, "Women Smuggled into U.S., Forced into Prostitution Try to Recoup $1 Million," *Palm Beach Daily*, April 8, 1999.

"Not in This Country, They Can't," Editorial, *The Washington Post*, January, 7, 1999.

Reports and Papers

Ad Hoc Committee on the Elaboration of a Convention against Transnational Organized Crime, revised draft Protocol to Prevent, Suppress and Punish Trafficking in Persons, especially Women and Children, Supplementing the United Nations Convention against Transnational Organized Crime, Fourth Session, Vienna, June 28-July 9, 1999.

Coalition Against Trafficking in Women, Trafficking in Women and Prostitution in the Asia Pacific, 1996.

Congressman George Miller and the Democratic Staff of the House Committee on Resources, "Beneath the American Flag: Labor and Human Rights Abuses in CNMI," March 26, 1998.

Foundation Against Trafficking in Women, International Human Rights Law Group, Global Alliance Against Traffic in Women, "Human Rights Standards for the Treatment of Trafficked Persons," 1999.

Federal Bureau of Investigation, Asian Criminal Enterprise Unit, Trafficking of Asian Aliens, July 1998

Global Survival Network, "Trapped: Human Trafficking for Forced Labor in The Commonwealth of the Northern Mariana Islands, a U.S. Territory," 1999.

Global Survival Network, "Crime and Servitude: An Exposé of the Traffic in Women for Prostitution from the Newly Independent States," October 1997.

Hughes, Donna, and Roche, Claire, Making the Harm Visible, Global Sexual Exploitation of Women and Girls, Coalition Against Trafficking in Women, Kingston, Rhode Island, February 1999.

Hughes, Donna, The Coalition Against Trafficking in Women, "Pimps and Predators on the Internet, Globalizing the Sexual Exploitation of Women and Children," Rhode Island, March 1999.

Human Rights Watch, United States, "Locked Away: Immigration Detainees in Jails in the United States," Vol. 10, No. 1, September 1998.

Immigration and Naturalization Service, Backgrounder on Trafficking Enforcement Case Summaries, October 23, 1998.

Immigration and Naturalization Service, Operation Lost Thai Special Report, September 28, 1999.

International Criminal Police Organization, (Interpol), Bird, Yoshi, "The Challenges Posed by Insufficient Collaboration and Communication in the Pro-Active Fight against Trafficking in Women, A Victim-Centered Approach to Anti-Trafficking Work," Lyon, France, September 1999.

Interpol, Bird, Yoshi, Draft copy, "The Trafficking of Children for Sexual Exploitation and Foreign Adoption: Background and Current Measures," Lyon, France, September 1999.

Interpol, International Conference on Trafficking in Women, Vienna, Austria 20 -October 21, 1998.

International Center for Migration Policy Development, "Draft Study on the Relationship Between Organised Crime and Trafficking in Aliens," Prepared by the Secretariat of the Budapest Group, Vienna, Austria, January 1999.

International Organization for Migration, "Feasibility Study on Rapid Information Transfer Aiming at Preventing and Combating Trafficking in Human Beings, in Particular Women and Children, for Sexual Exploitation in the European Union," European Commission, Task Force Justice and Home Affairs, STOP-Programme 1998/99.

International Organization for Migration, "Information Campaign Against Trafficking in Women From Ukraine," Project Report, July 1998.

International Organization for Migration, Subregional Office for East Asia and Oceania, Support to Trafficked and Other Vulnerable Women Migrant Workers in the Commonwealth of Northern Mariana Islands.

Israel Women's Network, Trafficking of Women to Israel and Forced Prostitution, November 1997.

Lederer, Laura, Dr., The Protection Project, "The Sex Trade: Trafficking of Women and Children in Europe and the United States, report for the Commission on Security and Cooperation in Europe," June 1999.

Lederer, Laura, Dr., The Protection Project—Creating an International Framework for Legislation to Protect Women and Children from Commercial Sexual Exploitation.

Information on the Legislation, Information on National and International Legislation Protecting Women and Children from Commercial Sexual Exploitation.

Miller, Ali and Stewart, Alison, International Human Rights Law Group, "Report from the Roundtable on The Meaning of Trafficking in Persons: A Human Rights Perspective," Women's Rights Law Reporter, Rutgers Law School, Fall/Winter 1998, Volume 20, Number 1.

Pilkerton, Chris, "Traffic Jam: Recommendations for Civil and Criminal Penalties to Curb the Recent Trafficking of Women from Post-Cold War Russia," Michigan Journal of Gender and Law, 1999.

Report of the Mission of the Special Rapporteur on Violence Against Women and Her Mission to Poland on the Issue of Trafficking and Forced Prostitution, May 24 - June 1997.

Skrobanek, Siriporn, Boonpakdi, Nattaya, Janthakeero, Chutima, The Traffic in Women, Human Realities of the International Sex Trade, Zed Book Ltd., London and New York, 1997.

The Hague, Ministerial Declaration on European Guidelines for Effective Measures to Prevent and Combat Trafficking in Women for the Purpose of Sexual Exploitation, Ministerial Conference, The Hague, April 24-26, 1997.

Trends in Organized Crime, *Special Focus*: Modern Slavery: Trafficking in Women and Children, Transnational Periodicals Consortium with the National Strategy Information Center, Summer 1998, Volume 3, Number 4.

UNIFEM, Trade in Human Misery, Trafficking in Women and Children, Asia Region, November 1998

United Nations, Report of the Secretary General, "Traffic in Women and Girls," September 1997.

UN Crime Commission: Report on the 6th Session of the UN Commission on Crime Prevention and Criminal Justice, April 1997.

State Department Cables

U.S. embassies around the world have reported on trafficking in women and children. Trafficking reports have been sent in from embassies in the following countries: Austria, Australia, Bangladesh, Belarus, Belgium, Brazil, Bulgaria, Burma, Canada, Czech Republic, Dominican Republic, Georgia, Greece, India, Indonesia, Ireland, Israel, Italy, Japan, Laos, Lithuania, Luxembourg, Malaysia, Moldova, Nepal, Nigeria, Pakistan, the Philippines, Poland, Romania, Russia, Singapore, Spain, South Korea, Sweden, Taiwan, Thailand, The Netherlands, The Vatican, Turkey, Turkmenistan, UAE, Ukraine, United Kingdom, and Vietnam.

Videos, Films, and Documentaries

Bruno, Ellen, "Sacrifice," Trafficking in Women and Girls in Southeast Asia, 1998.

Department of Justice, Office for Victims of Crime, "A Balance to Maintain," INS Informational Training Video.

Global Survival Network, "Bought and Sold," An Exposé of the Traffic in Women for Prostitution from the Newly Independent States, 1998.

Gupta, Ruchira, "The Selling of Innocents," Trafficking in Women and Girls in South Asia, December 1996.

Soki Paulin Ballesteros, International Organization for Migration, "Sex Trafficking: We're So Syndicated, Ma_am," public education video in the Philippines.

Transnational Seminar on Trafficking in Women, Budapest, June 1998.

Others

Attended the Global Conference on Trafficking and Sexual Exploitation, January 26-29, 1999, Dhaka, Bangladesh.

Debrief of a trafficking victim from the Czech Republic, New York, December 1998.

Debrief of a trafficker, West Palm Beach, Florida, April 1999.